# The Thesis
## Or Adventures in Academia

Marcus Rian

Books at Calliope Press
    *Musings*, Crawford Washington, Ed.
    *Masks*, Crawford Washington
    *Coyote Redux*, Violet Reason & Yulalona Lopez
    *Coyote Remasked*, Yulalona Lopez
    *Coyote Rebooted*, Yulalona Lopez
    *Coyote Reloaded*, Yulalona Lopez
    *Lucifer Dreaming*, Marcus Rian
    *Two Diaries*, Marcus Rian
    *Waiting for Better Times in Bulgaria*, Conor Ciaran

# The Thesis
## Or Adventures in Academia

Marcus Rian

Calliope Press/Mozart & Reason Wolf
Sarasota
2009

*Publication Information*

**Acknowledgments**: Cover photograph from University of Idaho archives (1983). Poetry from various works of A. M. Caratheodory, including *Amphibian Dreams* and *Masks*.

**Photographs**: Entrance to Adninistration Building 1976 (page 3), Library 1959 (6), Cant in the stacks (14), The bar in Cant's apartment (17), Cant's afro (18), Adninistration Building 1976 (20), Cant with Snakeman on glass (44), Walter & Gina 1976 (51), Cant after second hearing (57), Gymnasium lawn (62), Administration lawn (64), Can't's new apartment on Harrison (70), Gina painting in the kitchen on Second Street (84), Cant's portrait of Gina (92), Golf course run by observatory (108), Cant on bicycle at the Second Street apartment (120), Cant stacking wood for winter (135), Cant on Forest Survey (139), Cant with AH & M-P (146), Cant in Montana in Winter (149).

This Calliope Press Edition of THE THESIS
is Published by
Mozart & Reason Wolfe, Calliope Press
and marketed by 3 Muses Books

All rights reserved. Copyright © 1979 1999 2009 by
Marcus Rian under the International Union for the Protection of Literary and artistic works (Berne). Published in the United States by Mozart & Reason Wolfe, Ltd., Wilmington, Delaware

ISBN 0-911385-45-2
978-0-911385-45-8

Prepared and produced by Calliope Press, Sarasota
Designed by Rian Garcia Calusa Designs, Cortez

Please address all correspondence for the author, M&RW, Ltd., Calliope Press, Palouse Poets Collective, or Rian Garcia Calusa Designs to:
    editor@3musesbooks.com
    mozart@reasonwolf.com
    design@riangarciacalusa.com

## Contents

1. Idaho Hum   7
2. Stale Luck & Alien Dreams   17
3. The Power of Touch   18
4. The Metaphysics of Time   19
5. Wrestling with Monsters: Kneeling Before the Academic Hearing Board   21
6. Really Living, Going Running   44
7. Sewing Machines: Letter to the Student Newspaper   46
8. Words without Knowledge: Report of the Hearing Board   47
9. Making Love   50
10. Passionate Words to the President   52
11. Trees in Vats   58
12. The Committee of Three Meets Godzilla and Mothra   59
13. Going swimming   63
14. Desperate Words to the President   65
15. Moving Together   69
16. Numbers   71
17. The Epistemology of Plants   72
18. Found Art: Letter to the Student Newspaper   73
19. Two Mortals Visit God & an Archangle   74
20. Culture   81
21. Driving Around   85
22. A Sad Tale Sent to the Ancient Titans   86
23. Imitation   91
24. Standing before the Seated Faculty Council   93
25. Power   109
26. Proposed Faculty Honors: Letter to the Student Newspaper   110
27. Running at Night   112
28. Form without Substance: The Faculty Council Committee   113
29. Declaring Eternal Love   116
30. Epistle to the Jewel of the Gem State   117
31. Preparing for Exile   120
32. Another Facet, Another Reflection   121
33. Adjusting to Temporal Love   128
34. Misfits in Armor: An Open Letter to the University   130
35. Dream of Future Hell   132
36. In the Forest   134
37. Down to Georgia   142
38. Among the Pines   143
39. All Sweetness and Light   146
40. Eclipse of the Earth by the Moon   148

Dedications

To all the friends who asked questions and created good conversations. And, to all the students who never questioned their professors, and to all the professors that never questioned what or why they were teaching, and to all the administrators who never thought of questioning anything. And, to everyone who can laugh about their problems and have enough energy to dance.

The Library 1973

## 1. Idaho Hum

I abhor controversy, and I loathe participating in controversies of any kind, except for perhaps mild disagreements over book reviews. I am a Humanities Librarian at the Idaho Modern University in Simplotville, and I write book reviews for library journals. I never get involved in academic skirmishes. I was just a last minute fill-in as an academic advisor for Walter Cant, a graduate student in philosophy at the university—perhaps I shouldn't say philosophy exclusively, as Walter was an eager polymath, taking courses in astronomy, biology, anthropology, economics, and art, as well as his required courses. We spoke often about books that we were both reading. I found him to be an agreeable conversationalist. He also worked in the library, shelving books—after he finished reading many of them, of course. Even in the library, he learned as many things as possible, binding books one day and helping in cataloging the next.

I had no inkling that he was in trouble with his professors. How could he be? All he ever did was study, write, work—surely a boring existence for most people, although most amenable to people like myself, perhaps in spite of my husband's interest in social excitement. In any case, he came to me in mid-May, asking if I could fill in for his legal counsel, a third year law student at the university, at an appeal board meeting. I agreed, thinking an afternoon observing the elite of the academe make sophistic judgments would be an amusing break from the dry-balls of bookland.

The day before the big event, we met in the staff lounge of the library, which was decorated in the best 1950s style, and which was always deserted after the final afternoon break—all the more so, since the semester was to end the following day. There were two long blonde wooden tables in the center, surrounded by sturdy oak chairs. The north wall was all glass, making it very light during the day; it was light at night due to the six huge glass globes hanging from the ceiling. A coffee machine was on the table along the south wall. I went to it automatically for more coffee. I was wearing my uniform—dark skirt and coat, white blouse; he was wearing his—jeans, sweatshirt, and sneakers. Are they still called that? Sneakers? I didn't offer him anything; he only drank water. Our conversation was casual. He was certain that the board would find in his favor; I had no investment either way, beyond my two hours tomorrow.

"Here's my statement to the Hearing Board? Would you like to read it?" Walter asked.

"If you wish," I answered, "but perhaps you should tell me about your thesis first. I am acquainted with the general hopscotch procedure to land on the paper square."

"The thesis is an attempt to extend metaphysics through poetic language." He looked at me questioningly. I assumed he had neither played hopscotch nor finished a thesis.

"I suppose Aristotle would have trouble with that," I said.

"Aristotle was limited in his study of 'being' by his language."

"Aristotle was also one of the first to recognize the mathematical genius of Archytus, who invented the pulley, screw, and rattle, all important inventions for civilization."

"The rattle?"

"Kept children occupied so that they would not break things around the house, according to Aristotle. What philosopher is not linguistically limited?" I asked.

"Maurice Merleau-Ponty for one. His philosophy of Being was ambiguous, or rather his philosophy of ambiguity was unfinished—partly because of language, which he realized, and partly because of his death, which he probably didn't. My work is only a natural extension of his."

"So, why don't your professors like this work?" I asked. I started doodling, recombining the letters in his name, and making anagrams of new names. He was gazing at the ceiling, either assembling or remembering his sentences.

"Because, poetic expression is necessary to the subject—and none of them like poetry."

"So, why not write in prose?" I asked. The word cant was Latin for sing. Of course, in English it meant to talk in a hypocritical way, or to tilt suddenly.

"I am now," he admitted, "after several derailments, but some poetry is essential to the ideas."

"What is the title of the thesis?" I asked. I wondered, for the thousandth time, if people's names had anything to do with how they acted.

"It was 'Speaking and Silence' at first, then the 'Morphology of Being' for a while. Now it is the 'Metaphorical Excavation of the Flesh.'"

"Sounds faintly pornographic. Why change? Why not change it again?" I asked. I liked him. He was handsome in a classical Greek way, curly hair, straight nose, and athletic build, sort of like the description of Ludwig Wittgenstein. About Wittgenstein: After being received by Wittgenstein in his room for tea, J. N. Finally wrote: "he looked like Apollo who had bounded into life out of his own statue ... blue-eyed and fair-haired ... with a beauty that ... breathed the four Greek cardinal virtues." Walter was like that, but he seemed to lack the humor of the Greek Gods.

Walter continued: "Every time I understood more of Merleau-Ponty's thought, a change suggested itself. But not pornographic, no" he smiled. "Remember our discussion on pornography as a social crutch? 'Flesh' is a technical term by the way."

"I thought we agreed it was just a symptom of social unbalance—which is what a crutch does, oh never mind. So, how is he different from Aristotle? Or flesh from whatever?" Apollo, God of the Sun? I looked at him again. Maybe, maybe not—a little too much meanness around the lips.

"Aristotle based his metaphysics on a basic category, substance, whereas Merleau-Ponty began with the human body—"

"So Being with a capital B is the subject of the thesis" I asked. I finished rearranging the 'r-a-l.' I wondered if he knew that one of the anagrams for his name was 'weak central bit'? A bad sign for a philosopher-to-be. Well, maybe not—processing is not as important as memory in philosophy.

"Yes, I want to investigate the possibility of describing the ground of existence, Being. Aristotle defined the problem, but was unable to solve the ambiguity of Being-as-universal, or Being-as-individual, using his critical method of analysis."

"And that's where Merleau-Ponty comes in, I would guess." Maybe he looked more like Debussy, the French composer. I myself resemble someone famous, but I can never remember who since I never watch her movies. Katherine Hepburn, perhaps.

"Yes, Merleau-Ponty began existentially with the human body instead of relying on some substance. Perception is a direct access to Being. Perception is the primary activity of the body in the world, then expression. Expression is embodied in perception, as perception is in the body, as the body is in the world. Verbal expression transforms Being through the creation of ideal symbols. Language makes Being visible in an ideal system."

"Wait, why not just use Aristotle's language, then?" I understood him to mean that everything was embodied in some embodiment. Still sounded pornographic.

"It is inadequate for a complete presentation of Being. Art and other expressions are inadequate avenues to Being, also, owing to the fundamental ambiguity of limited perspectives. Merleau-Ponty proposed a creative language for metaphysics, but died before he could carry it out."

"So that's what you're trying to do."

"Exactly! Poetry is necessary to awaken the power of expression, to transcend things already said. The thesis offers a phenomenological interpretation of poetry and the mechanics of metaphor, based on the radical philosophy of Merleau-Ponty. Of course, others have done similar things, so I examine some of the works of philosophers who wrote in poetic form. I conclude, and here is the difference, that both poetry and philosophy are needed to attempt to grasp Being. Poetry requires the hyper-reflective awareness of philosophy, and philosophy must use the lateral approach of poetry; poetic philosophy, a speaking that carries beyond the limits of physical world and language, is suggested as the most adequate expression for metaphysics."

"And that's what you said? And that's what the committee objects to? Just skimming through the first chapter, I notice a lot of questions that I presume you will answer." Another anagram for his name was 'we bracket Latin', very appropriate for a philosopher.

"Basically. But it's not a linear path leading to a definite conclusion; it's a dialectical spiral that requires the creative effort of a reader to be put together. If thesis asks more questions than it answers, it is for the purpose of stimulating even more questions. I don't think it even asks enough questions. The committee also objects that it obscure. If it is obscure, it may be so because its subject is, or its expression is; it attempts to say that which possibly cannot be said."

"So, you're trying to say something that may not be possible to say to a committee that possibly cannot hear, and you want a bigger committee of academic nuisances to hear you say it? The hearing may not be enough." I sighed. I hate to see people try to be original in a university setting. I skimmed through a few of the earlier chapters. Walter started making notes on his statement to the Board. "I notice there's a whole section on thermodynamics and entropy. These didn't seem to be poetic topics. I assume you have integrated that somehow."

"Sure."

"I've now read—more precisely caused my eyes to gaze upon—several pages of your thesis and reluctantly conclude—reluctantly because I'm aware of your desire to have a thoughtful response—that my indoctrination at the hands of philosophy professors considered to be versed in such metaphysical matters was considerably less than needed to prepare me to converse with you in depth. Also, you managed to avoid saying how entropy had anything to do with being."

"Oh, yes, sorry. I am rewriting the Intro—that will be part of it. As for entropy, it is a characteristic of Being, along with 'ektropy.' I bring it in to link philosophical thinking with physics, to describe entropy poetically as well."

"How do you do that?"

"Using the metaphor of turning. By showing—

"Yes, maybe later. I notice mythology and ethics. Don't you think that's too much. That you should trim the thing, you know, minimize it?"

"I have somewhat, but that's why I like philosophy. It's a license to study anything. Philosophy is the only thing that can study every thing. It's pure wondering. Maybe the outcome of this wondering is not a kind of knowledge at all, but understanding. Maybe Socrates was right, philosophy is just an attitude. One that lets you continue in the face of ignorance."

I knew about Socrates. He was the founder of the educational quiz game. He was able to drink all other philosopher/playwrights under the table, even Aristophanes. Ugly as a satyr, gentle as a cupid. A midwife to the birth of ideas. He was a sculptor by trade but ignored the quiet demands of his business and the shrill demands of his wife. His philosophy was know thyself, *Gnothi seauton*, that process which let us know ourselves. Socrates was famous for his courage in battle, for defending an admiral accused of cowardice, for defying the tyrant Critias, and finally for submitting to death for corrupting the youth by turning them to philosophy. After this thoughtful digression, I responded: "But philosophy as an attitude. Your professors won't want to hear that, I'm sure." I thought: Philosophy is knowledge with an attitude, wow. Hope the college kids don't find that out.

"It isn't possible to be more exact. It isn't a science. We know we exist; we know we are made of flesh. In the *Physics*, Aristotle said that to 'seek proof of matters, for which we already possess clearer evidence than any proof can afford, is to confuse the better with the worse.' The metaphysical data is elementary evidence: The questioning being exists, has a body, carries the past within, deliberates the future, and changes over time. When this data conflicts with our beliefs, a problem is formed to which a metaphysical theory responds with a solution. To be wise a philosopher must suspend judgment of the final truth of things; theories are to be held loosely, in spite of valid proofs or contradictions. Being may be pure actuality, or the mind may be independent of the body. What is the final basis of philosophical knowledge? How is it reached? Is it reachable? The philosopher cannot know for sure. Philosophy is therefore something questionable, as well as a questioning."

"Well, stop presenting the turgid stuff of lectures would you? And stop stringing hypothetical, I mean rhetorical, questions together. Ordinary words, even old dried metaphors, are good enough. Why did you start with all this psychology? Why not start at the beginning?" I saw that the history of being was mid-way through the contents.

"Because, as M-P says, that there are no principal problems,"

"Who's MP? Military Police?"

"No, but that's good. Merleau-Ponty. The problems—they are all concentric; what is first for us is not necessarily what is first as such. Philosophy must move, therefore, from that which is first for us to that which is first as such, and even then it must be resigned to being limited to that first in itself that is already present in what is first to us. How does that philosophy reach the very beginnings which determine it, when even a farmer cannot see that part of the field on which he is standing? All philosophies circle about the beginnings; some attempt to reach and comprehend them, but have difficulties, due to the unrelatedness of their beautiful order, as in Spinoza, or to their disorder, as in Nietzsche. I just chose to start with what I knew, like Descartes and M-P."

"Is that what Merleau— M-P, did?"

"M-P's philosophy is a radical phenomenology. The beginning is initially presented in order to convince and sustain thought in a circular fashion toward itself; this circling then moves in a spiral turning toward the beginnings of philosophy and finally the ultimate beginnings. In his last writings, he begins to search for the basis of the dimensions of expression—that which makes sense of the world. This dimension upon which all experience and intelligibility depend is 'flesh'—also referred to as Being, or being as being. Flesh is a technical term coined by Merleau Ponty to emphasize that everything, ideas and bodies, is incarnate in Being."

"Oh." It wasn't going to be pornographic.

"His later work tries to restore the world as a meaning of Being—to present wild Being as the primordial meaning of Being. This wild Being that can never be exhausted, or even posited, is the perceptual world. Philosophy attempts to uncover the latent intelligibility in the sensible world by taking it up in expression and forming it into ideas. Paradoxically, philosophical thought enters existence through expression; as philosophy interrogates language and thought it finds that it is interrogating itself. Philosophy is then a descriptive disclosure of the strangeness of the world through the detours of language, hence itself. Its task is to show the invisible in order to unconceal it. This can only be done with a creative language."

"And poetry is that expression?" Maybe it would be pornographic. Too many rhetorical questions, again, but at least some were answered right away.

"Yes, Heidegger came to the same conclusion. He wrote that to recognize the ontological difference between Being and beings is to think poetically, and to forget it is to be condemned to metaphysics—oddly, he wrote conceptually and directly to the issue, and had to admit failure. Others, from the pre-Socratics to Santayana, have tried poetry with varying degrees of success."

"Heidegger—that reminds me of a story..." I fumbled with my memory. "Heidegger used his philosophy to support National Socialism, Nazism, thinking that it was moving in a proper direction for the relationship of humanity and technology. Because Nazism was consistent with his own views, he recognized its inner truth and 'greatness.' Democracy and scientific progress were just the dying embers of the original Greek error in philosophy according to Heidegger. Nazism was the radical revolution needed to restore the order lost. Heidegger and Hitler proclaimed a need to return to a natural order—return to the blood and soil, blut und ... something German. The funny thing is, in his rejection of Aristotle and Darwin, Heidegger concluded that humans are not animals, even rational animals. This lead to a real contradiction, as he had to espouse the same anthropocentrism and dualism that characterized the Greek tradition of metaphysics he was trying to replace. Even 20 years after the war, he believed that Nazism had potential." I took a deep breath.

"But, wait a minute, Heidegger's idea of 'caring' which 'lets things be'—this can't be the same as Hitler's application of the stern laws of nature. I'll have to look that up. How do you know so much about Hitler? If Heidegger was an unrepentant Nazi, maybe I shouldn't use him as a source?"

"No," I reassured him, "the ideas are considered separate from the political activities. You can use the ideas without prejudice." I was thinking of my old professor Hans Henry Vane, who spent years studying Nazi art and history in the

Nazi Archive bunker outside of Denver. The attraction of the world for the Nazis has not diminished after 50 years. The thousand year reign may only be of a few ideas that will not ever go away.

"Are they separate? I'm not so sure. Perhaps it would be better, as the Greeks did, to refine the ideas of others and then not give credit to the original unrefined thought."

"Well, just footnote him for now, or remove him. Do you need him?"

"His ideas support my position. I'll use him."

"Okay. Let's sum up. I have a book review to do."

"What book?"

"Later," I was eager to have dinner at five. With all the intellectual disorder around me, I found it was necessary to have a few strict habits, dietary and otherwise.

"Let me just read the summary, then," he said almost pleading: 'This thesis explores the reasons why poetry must be used in the discussion of Being, and it uses the philosophy of Merleau-Ponty as the basis for explanation. However, the thesis is not a systematic attempt to form a coherent theory from M-P; he did not even offer a system, claiming that metaphysics is the opposite of a system. Whether a system is even possible is questionable, since it might be antithetical to the subject: Being as invisible, or the realm of possibility. This thesis also intertwines poetic forms with prose forms to be adequate for the subject. If statements seem to be repeated, or discussion moves in circles, the intention was to create an ontological spiral. As M-P defines Being, it must be reached indirectly to be redefined; the passage to the foundation of the world is a spiral. It is an allusive expression, a texture of thought woven from the dense fibers of the body and the light tendrils of the mind, both of which are embodied in the flesh of the world. The study of Being is a metaphorical excavation of the flesh.' "

"Where does this page go?" I asked, looking over it. "I'm not sure I want to offer an opinion so ill-formed as to merit your intellectual scorn or possibly social rebuff." He waved his hand and started reading from the last page.

" 'The philosopher is confronted with the whole universe, that is, everything, but he—or she—cannot stand before it like a physicist before a circuit, nor even state it circumspectly like a sociologist with a social group; she is limited to making a vague gesture—towards everything there is—and realizing that most of it by necessity is unknown. The philosopher really cannot know what the entire object of his study is; because it is whole, it is that which cannot be given as an object, and because it is not given, it is a questioning whose answers are perennially sought. For this reason, philosophical knowledge is never complete. Instead philosophy is an attempt to attain a complete perspective, to fill in the constellations on a cloudy night, or map lands beyond a horizon; scientific knowledge is exact, but incomplete—it of necessity is embedded in a complete and ultimate something, which is always somewhat unreachable, and tempting in its remoteness. Philosophy is then a hungry questioning after the attitude of the universe and the meaning of life: Stars are the thoughts of night, Heine wrote, restless and golden; philosophy is an expression of wonder at them, as well as an attempt to read them.' That's for the Intro.," he said.

"Okay, take out a few commas for dependent clauses. I've read the summary of your case to the Hearing Board while you were expounding your exegesis. I think it is adequate, if too hydra-headed." Your epexegetic exegesis surfeit with bombastic neologisms, I thought.

"How do you mean?"

"You're questioning too much: university procedures, form, the adequacy of the thesis, and perhaps the competence of your professors. As you know the stakes in academia are so low that the fighting is bound to be vicious. Can you limit the focus of your appeal, say to the merits of the work?" I hoped he would.

Writing rapidly, he started talking without looking up. "I find 'three problems with the acceptance of my thesis by my Masters Committee:

1. They approved it, but later changed their minds.
2. They directed numerous and contradictory changes in style, and
3. They made numerous and contradictory changes in the content.

In spite of their changes, I believe that the thesis is comparable to others in the department and college, and it deserves to be formally awarded a Masters degree.' What do you think?"

"Better. Keep it shorter and leave out some of the flowery justification." I looked for my coat. "I do hope that the project will live, but if it does end up in dispute after this I'm sure you will have little difficulty mastering the wretched brains of twelve honest persons."

He looked at me quizzically. "I don't see how, but I'll emphasize the work itself. Thank you for your time. See you tomorrow at 1:00."

Walter in the Stacks

## 2 Stale Luck & Dream Aliens

Just a year ago, everything had seemed so promising. After I left Seattle, with $40 left to my name, I drove east to Simplotville, Idaho. The first evening in Simplotville, I stayed at the New Idaho Hotel and had dinner. I was the only one in the quite nice dining room. The next day I found an apartment in an old garage on Washington Street (for $25 a month); the people who lived in the house were an anthropologist and a geologist. I sold the car for $50.00 to the American Motors dealer. I went over to the university and talked to people in biology, psychology, physics, philosophy, and forestry. Then I stopped by the state employment department.

The second day, the department of philosophy accepted me as a conditional graduate student. I could start taking courses in two weeks; I agreed to take two directed studies.

The third day, I got in a veteran's program with state employment; they would pay 75 percent of my salary. I interviewed with the head of the university library, who fancied himself a polymath—we got along quite well, as I also fancied myself one. He offered me a job as a book shelver, to start in a week. The senior secretary Calegina was polite and very attractive.

The summer days were wonderful. I woke up with the sun and went for walks, before going to work and classes. The yard was filled with birds and cats; the room was filled with mice and roaches—the downside of living in an old garage. The summer went by quickly. I studied hard. I started running with one of the professors, who invited me to move into his new house (in the basement); we went running everyday.

With my regular income, I bought some new clothes at the Yellow Front and at Goodwill—great useless things like brown suede shoes with four-inch heels (now I am well over six feet tall at last!). I spent several coffee breaks hanging around the secretary.

Then Gina and I fell in love and that seemed to complete a perfect year for me. We communicated through notes left in the astronomy part of the reference section—not many people knew how to use it. Today, I had left a note for Gina in the library, asking her to meet me tomorrow, after the appeal.

I was more tired than I thought. Every day of this semester had added to the burden. I biked back to my underground lair and fixed a snack of peanut butter and apricot jam on the sunflower seed bread. I went into the bathroom and washed the dishes. The apartment had a bar with a large closet in the living room, where I kept my clothes. I had made some bar stools out of 2x12s and I had an old Danish couch next to them. There was a little storage room that I had made into a study; it was next to the small bath with a shower, which is where I washed the dishes; we became clean at the same time. I listened to music for an hour, writing at the bar, and then turned out the light. I had to quiet the brain, so I could sleep.

The last dream: I am at one of Joe Jackson's bungalows: it is a one-story, glass-block house on a hill, with flat-roofed carport. I find pieces of notes on the ground; they have my name on them. Someone has followed me and he says his name is Brian; he is investigating a murder in the area. Then we hear a car. I say walk down to the road. The car comes around the corner and up the driveway.

It is a large light green 3-door Buick of 1963 vintage. Joe is driving; 3 men are riding. They all get out. I hail Joe and tell him we are looking for a murder site across the road, when I noticed his name on the mailbox. He picks up all the papers with my name on them, there is one left on the ground. One of the large men picks it up and gives it to me. It is handwritten. Not important. I put it in my pocket and say we are leaving. Joe waves.

We cross the street and start downhill towards a lake, surrounded by small houses and a trailer court. As we pass the small driveway entrance to the court, Brian hurries in. I get lost, but then see him in the center of a group of seated people. So I sit lower across the path. An older woman sits down beside me; there are 5 empty seats on each side of me but she chooses the one on my left. She is slim, straight, white-haired and seems blind, so I tell her what is happening; she says don't bother thank you as she is not deaf.

I see Brian leave, and then my consciousness splits in two and I am with him also. He goes to a dock and finds the body of the murder victim in back of the work shed in a pile of fishing nets. He/I hear a noise and dive behind the body and into a pile of nets. A small man swims up to the nets and looks around, stares at the body, sniffs the air, and goes into the shed.

At the trailer park meeting, the small piece of paper from Joe has become a series of photos; my brothers Shane and Ted and three others are in a convertible with the top down. I am in one or two. There are two of the murder victim, which I shuffle to the bottom. The woman asks me about them, so I talk about a few. She talks about Providence and Boston, where some of the pictures were taken. She had gone to Brown and frequented the Athenaeum library in Providence. We talk about places, books and ideas. She asks about the crime. I say I know nothing.

Because I know about Brian, I decide to walk across the road to the work shed. I excuse myself, but the woman wants to walk along. I shrug and say okay. It is really night by now and dark. We cross the road and go into the shed. From there we can see two figures patrolling the area. I see at least one body. I take the woman's arm and say we must go.

She runs surprisingly fast ahead of me, but stops at the first building up the hill, another work shed, two story, wood. She opens the door and goes in.

# The Thesis

I follow. We hear a voice and go up wooden stairs, see a small light. Suddenly someone in front of us asks who we are what we want. I say we need to call the police about a crime. He nods and we walk over to a desk. He says he cannot find the phone, but to wait there. A noise and voices. She rushes behind the stairs, which go up to a loft. I stand behind her. A chain lift brings up a body bag with the two men I had seen at the work shed. They see us immediately and take us downstairs. They take us behind some pallets; one of them turns into a large snake and tries to strike me. I push his head away each time. The fight pushes me outside. I see the body of Brian in the nets.

Tired, I sit on a box. The snake man is joined by the other. I wonder if the woman is dead. The other is a snake and they separate to attack me, one from each side. I keep batting their heads away. A third person come out, the fellow from the shed. He says he is sorry he has to kill me. I say he doesn't. I am just a writer. I give my word never to reveal the murders or the killers. He says that will never work. I say give me back my 'girlfriend' and I will never talk. He looks confused and talks with one of the others in a hissing dialect. The other two have changed into serpent dogs and are trying to bite me, sliding along the wall, under nets and around barrels. They stop. The woman comes out with a fourth man. He lets her go.

We walk up the road a ways and sit on a log. In the dawn now she seems to have fewer wrinkles. I look closely at her and ask her why she didn't kill me. She smiles and says she only wanted to know, at first what I knew, later what I thought of our conversation. I ask her what shape she is naturally. She says that is not important. She just wanted to know why I tried to protect her. I ask why the first victim was murdered and why the detective, Brian. She says that is not important for me to know, then asks if she can trust me. I say yes, I gave my word, even if it was for the wrong reason. I stand up. She steps to me and hugs me; I feel too many ribs. I ask her if she will walk with me. She says, a ways. So, we walk and talk about existence. I ask her if I will see her again. She says maybe and runs away, much too sure and fast for a blind woman, much too graceful for a human. I say after her departing form that I will be in the library next Tuesday.

I am exhausted, but walk up the hill until I can walk no more, then sleep on the sidewalk until the first of the sun strikes me.

The Basement Apartment Bar

*3 The Power of Touch*

The following day, I got to the Library early to finish some work before the big appeal. I found that Gina had already left me a note, so I read it: "I believe that you will topple their arguments like dominoes and trip them like wooden, poke-a-dotted, serious, vain-glorious, cardboard cut-outs." A good message.

I was shelving books when she came into the stacks. I was sitting on a stool, reading a book on astronomy, when she saw me. I got up, guiltily, although I had finished placing the entire cart. She paid no attention and kissed me intently. I lowered my arms under her buttocks and raised her above me, so I could open her blouse from the bottom with my lips.

She struggled, laughing lightly, and said, "Put me down. Please." Well, it was the please that broke my concentration. She said, as she smoothed her blouse, "Bad time, we both have to have clean clothes for the afternoon."

"Oh, another meeting?" I asked.

"Oh, just the Newsletter group." She smiled playfully and lifted her blouse and bra up to her neck. I automatically lifted my shirt and we lightly rubbed. "That is such a wonderful ritual," she said, "but we need to keep it mostly for home."

"That was the best encouragement I could have," I said honestly. "I just hope I can concentrate on the thesis, now."

"Oh, you'll be fine, they're just perfessers."

She went back downstairs, flipping her skirt a little.

I pulled my hair to the sides, so it looked a little like an afro, and sighed like a truck with broken air brakes.

After a few more hours of work, I went downstairs to Ellsin's office, to see if she was ready.

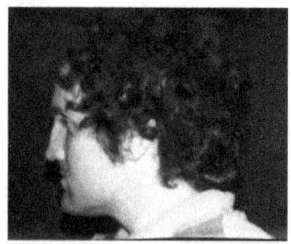

Cant's Quick Afro

# 4 The Metaphysics of Time

"What time is it!?" I asked too loudly, as I entered her glass office.

"Twoish, maybe," Ellsin shrugged.

"What time do we need to meet?"

"Did you ever realize how stupid clocks are?" she asked.

"I just assumed it had to do with the sun."

"People time was solar. Babylonians and Hindus, as Aborigines, Desana, and Masai, calculated their day from sunrise. Athenians and Jews, Orthodox Moslems, began their day at sunset, often setting the clock to 12," she finally looked up from her notes.

"So clocks were solar devices?" I asked not wanting to have this conversation, but curious about where it was heading.

"No, they came out of a religious orientation to life. The world view of the Benedictine monasteries of the twelfth century produced the first real mechanical clock. The idea was to produce regularity to daily routines. So, some monks would not pray too much, so others would not work too long transcribing books or growing grapes. The monasteries required seven periods of devotion during the day. The bells were rung at first to signal canonical hours. The mechanical clock was developed to give more precision to time for rituals.

"But, the clock kept track of other hours. It allowed all activities to become synchronized. By the Fourteenth century, people in towns used mechanical clocks. It brought regularity to working people and merchants. In 1370, Charles V of France ordered the citizens of Paris to regulate commercial, industrial, and probably private life to the bells of the Royal Palace clock, which struck every 60 minutes. Churches had to change their bells from canonical hours to regular civil hours.

"Thus a thing invented by religious people, dedicated to devotion, became more useful to those devoted to the accumulation of money. The clock made capitalism possible. It made mass production possible. It made wage slavery possible. Lewis Mumford claimed that it also made possible the idea of regular production, regular working hours, and regular (standard) products. Clocks also made computers possible."

"Hey, the school just got a new computer."

"Sigh, quantification. But, clocks. The word 'clok' came from the Dutch word for bell. The word day came from the Saxon word to 'burn.' The word hour from Greek meaning season or twelfth part of the sun. But, to get to 24, the Babylonians had numbers based on 60. They and Egyptians had 24 hours per day and 360 (+5) days per year. Thus a circle had 360 degrees."

Walter started to tune out of the conversation. He actually wanted to think about swimming, how to improve his stroke, or even the looming trial of his thesis.

"Even though our time is linear, other people thought of time as rhythmic, oscillating time, cyclic, zig-zag, or spiral—"

He coughed quietly, trying not to be obvious. "We are, alas, on linear, absolute, nuclear time—"

She looked up and said smoothly, "That time already? Okay, let's go."

Philosophy Department Third floor left of center

## 5 Wrestling with Monsters: Kneeling Before the Academic Hearing Board

When we arrived, only the Sound Technician was there, so we talked to her, or rather I did, since Walter was crossing out paragraphs in his appeal statement. The hearing was on the third floor of the Administration Building, a 1900s gothic monster with sixteen-foot ceilings and polished maple floors—polished as if by thousands of rear-ends being pulled across it on blankets, reminding me of my basic training in the Air Force. When they opened an old base in Amarillo to basic training, the barracks needed cleaning. The first class, therefore, spent all its time waxing floors, in fact using the rear end method since there were only two floor machines, and painting walls for the other classes who would, instead of learning janitorial skills, be trained in the more manly arts of death and destruction—it couldn't have been discrimination against women. The wainscoting was a dark wood, like walnut. The lamp globes were 1950s replacements. The ancient white of the walls echoed the words of our conversation and gave them a more solemn tone than the subject demanded. The girl was in electrical engineering. Two students came, friends of Walters perhaps, although they didn't look at him. The board members dribbled in in clumps, the chairman in the last group. Walter went over to speak with him.

"Professor Dodd? My name is Walter Cant. My advisor had to cancel this morning and couldn't make it, so this is Ellsin Moon from the Library, who will bear witness for me."

"Yes, hello. Sorry I'm late." Dodd looked like Don Knotts or one of those actors hired for meek parts, hunched over from sitting or from carrying the weight of his world, with perhaps a pinch of scholarly confidence.

"How will you run the meeting, by the book?" Walter asked, plunging seriously into the jaws of academic death.

"No, I prefer a simple informal meeting, if you don't mind."

Walter did: "As long as we follow Robert's Rules in the main. What is the function of the Academic Hearing Board by the way? Do you have the power to recommend action?"

"Well," paused Dodd, "I—I'm not sure. Is that a copy of the Faculty Handbook there with your papers? Let me look it up."

"Everyone is here," Dean Hard stated. Everyone was: a dumpy frau, must be from home ec, two older, proudly grey, administrative types, and two nondescript males in their 40s. The committee of three had come in as a unit. Professor Finn I recognized from the city school board meetings, tall and impressive, but with a head slightly too small for the big-boned body. Professor Carson, with her splendidly big hair, from a giant beaver or possibly from the beard of the early Karl Marx, falling down the back of her long-waisted body; nice eyes, I thought. And Professor Kraft, sort of Burt Reynoldsy pot-bellied with the hair from a cherub in a fresco, only dark brown.

"Perhaps we should begin then," Dodd acknowledged. "Could you turn on the tape machine, young man? Thank you. I will start."

Dodd: This is a formal hearing of the Academic Hearing Board convened on May 15, 1975, to hear an appeal from Mr. Walter Bike Cant, a graduate student in the Philosophy Department, concerning his Master's thesis. The Board, quoting from the University Handbook says, only when the Academic Hearing Board has found that the petitioner has been denied a fair hearing, that regular, departmental, or college procedures have not been followed, or that the decision now appealed was discriminatory with respect to the petitioner, The decision of the Academic Hearing Board shall determine whether any academic regulation or requirement has been met or shall be waived. The members of the Board present today are: the Chairman, Reginald L. Dodd, speaking, Professors Bert J. Sooner, Mars Holland, Lisa O'dell. The student member of the committee is not in attendance. Also present is Assistant Dean Hard from the Graduate School who is here in the status as an observer. Also present are Professor Caesar Sam Finn, and Professor Leigh I. Carson, and Professor K. Ronn Kraft, who constitute the Graduate Committee for Mr. Cant.

The procedure that the committee is going to follow—Mr. Cant will first present his supporting information for his complaint, then Dr. Carson will present her rebuttal, then Professor Finn, and then Professor Kraft, if he has anything to add. At that point, the various parties will be allowed to cross-question each other. The evidencery part of the hearing, or after the evidencery part of the hearing, the Board will retire and deliberate, and make its judgment in private. And then, all participants will be notified by mail, as soon as possible, of the Academic Hearing Board's decision. Mr. Cant, are you ready to proceed?

Sooner: Reg, there's another, Mrs. Moon, present.
Moon: May I add that for posterity, that Professor Ellsin Moon is present.
Dodd: Ellsin Moon, from the Library, is present and I—you're his —
Moon: I'm representing council —
Dodd: Council —
Moon: Moral support, et cetera. (Was I in another dimension? The universe of slow people?)
Dodd: Okay. For whom?
Moon: Walter Cant. (I was, dear God, could I reach the portal in time?)
Cant: You're here to witness the sacrifice.
Dodd: Okay, Mr. Cant, if you're ready, you can proceed.

Cant: Thank you. I thought before I really started reading my complaint, that I would muddy the issue as much as possible, hopefully so that all of you would think that when I finish my presentation, it will be that much more clear compared to the preface. I had assumed when I became a graduate student, that there were fairly defined rules as regards the relationship between the major professor and the student, and the student and the rest of his committee. But recently, in reading through the Faculty Handbook, I was unable to find any guidelines at all. Certainly, there don't seem to be any formal guidelines as to the number of drafts or the length of the draft. In my own discussions with various professors and graduate students, and of course, Dean Strand, I found that the upper limit for drafts seems to be somewhere around two or three, and that most students as soon as they submit their first rough draft receive editorial comments from their professor and then prepare the final draft. I know this is true in Art, and Chemical Engineering, and Physics, at least.

There also seems to be no definition of what a thesis is. Since I work in the Library, all the theses that are bound eventually come through my hands to be put on the shelves, or carded, and I make a habit of reading through them. And it seems to me, that book reports and original research, and oh, I don't know, what shall we say, just other types of reports and some creative endeavors all seem to make their way into the Library as theses.

I also could not find any evidence of what the professor's response to a thesis was supposed to be. Is the professor obligated to even read it? As far as I know, from hearsay evidence, normally most members of the committee do not even read or attempt to read the thesis. The major professor reads it, and the thesis is typed, and it's sent in. And this is true, I know, in Chemical Engineering and Physics, at least. So, I'm slightly confused as to the extent of the professor's responsibility in helping the student prepare.

In forming my committee a year ago, I asked Dr. Carson to be my major professor, and she agreed. Dr. Carson recommended or approved the rest of the committee. As far as I know, all of the procedures in the Graduate Student Bulletin, on page 47, were followed. Over parts of the summer and fall, he helped me outline my program and approved it. Well, actually, this began in January of '74, when we—I began to take a directed study in the phenomenology of Maurice Merleau-Ponty. Well, after quite a number of detours in style and length, I completed a final draft. In accord with his directions, I finished the thesis, and I was told that it would be signed. I had been told by Dr. Finn, that he would sign anything that Dr. Carson would sign, and Professor Kraft that he would sign anything the other two would sign, and I had been told by Dr. Carson that she would sign it—and Dr. Carson told at least two other students, Lease and Baltimore, with whom I have talked, that she would also sign it on April 2nd.

After a reversal of opinion in which Dr. Finn convinced Dr. Carson that it wasn't ready to be signed, I took the problem to Dean Strand, who suggested that he attempt to discuss the matter with Dr. Carson and Dr. Finn, who apparently decided that if he Dr. Finn went alone to see Dean Strand, Dean Strand could be convinced that there was really no problem at all. After this, Dean Strand suggested that I petition through him, the Academic Hearing Board to convene. This was done on the, I believe, 3rd of April. Dean Strand wrote his letter to the Board sometime between the 7th and the 18th of April, and the Board, after a number of delays and changes of time, has met. Since all the normal procedures were followed, and I think I can show this, and all the requisite work, course work, and thesis work has been completed, I want to ask this Board to decide that the requirements had been met.

The thesis was done as Dr. Carson directed, in spite of those inconsistencies and often ambiguous comments. And on April 2nd, she approved it and accordingly told myself and others of that fact. I was instructed to hire a typist and to that end, Dr. Carson helped me to prepare the manuscript by indicating what things should be changed to facilitate typing. And with Dr. Carson's permission, I did hire a typist, and I had to get the manuscript back from her, since I was told that I could not go on without everyone's permission. Throughout her examination of the thesis, Dr. Carson rarely, if ever, found any conceptual or theoretical errors. Equally rare were any spelling or grammatical errors.

At Dr. Finn's insistence, the first draft, which was basically a rehash of a paper done in May of '74 for Dr. Carson's directed study, was typed by a secondary school English teacher. Dr. Finn read the first three pages and indicated that, in his opinion, I had no conversant knowledge of Plato or Aristotle, and that, he was unqualified to read the remaining 39 or so pages of the paper in typed form. He even objected when I used Plato's real name Platon— Plato was just a nickname because of his broad shoulders.

Plato had an interesting life. Plato's desire was to see 'rightness' established in society. Despite his time as an exile, then philosopher-slave, Plato spent the last years of his life teaching quietly in a garden. He died taking a nap at the wedding feast of one of his students.

Umm, let me see. Oh yes. Several other drafts were typed by the senior secretary of the Library, who is also a graduate English student and a former copy editor, and the final draft, which Dr. Finn magnanimously offered to allow his secretary to type, was typed by several of the departmental secretaries. Various drafts of the thesis and parts of it have also been read by Professors in the Library, Physics, Chemistry, Music, Architecture, Anthropology, Psychology, and if Dr. Kraft read any of it, Art (laughs). Oh, Professor Kraft, my apologies. Dr. Carson, after changing her mind, communicated to me verbally that he disliked the style of only perhaps 10 percent of the thesis, and that, that was the reason for his retraction of approval, and that was the reason that he felt he could not defend it at all, before Professor Finn and Professor Kraft, who had read less than probably 10 pages each within the past ten months. I would like to contend that style cannot be adequate reason for denying a thesis. Dr. Carson's amazing inconsistency is not typical of her, nor is it normal departmental procedure. For instance, while she— I was waiting for her to read the 6th draft of my thesis, I asked her if he could read it right away and she said, no, she was working on the 1st draft of Eric Rhodes's thesis—Rhodes is also a Master's candidate in Philosophy—and that she was having to rewrite the whole thing because of Mr. Rhodes's faulty English. Apparently after that, the draft was corrected or given to everyone else in that committee, and according to Professor Finn's secretary, Helen, the committee read, corrected, and approved the entire thesis in one day.

Generally speaking, I don't think its at all compatible with the concept of standard Master's thesis course as outlined in the Faculty Handbook—I lost my place, huh! Huh—to alter the style repeatedly throughout six of the seven drafts without really changing the substance at all. Furthermore, to withhold the degree due to the—some arbitrary designation of style alone, goes against the function of the University itself, to restrict a student to an echo of a professor's style, or at least his, ah, shall we say, standardization of a style, is to deny the aspirations which the University itself lists in its own Handbook, that is to imbue the Mind with knowledge, tolerance, and vision. This type of behavior be a faculty—by faculty members would tend to stifle creativity instead of ever encouraging it. Also, according to the faculty professional ethics, professors recognize the responsibilities placed on them, and as teachers, they are to encourage "the free pursuit of learning in a student." They are to "demonstrate respect for the student as an individual and adhere to their proper role as intellectual guide and counselor."

I was wondering what kind of guidance I've actually been given. Dr. Finn has rewritten the first three pages five times, and at the end of that time, he's told me, after correcting his own corrections, that it was satisfactory in substance. When I talked with Dean Strand afterwards, Dr. Finn, according to Dean Strand, had told him, meaning Dean Strand, that none of it was satisfactory at all, none of those three pages. Dr. Finn then also tends to label me temperamental if I dislike or fail to incorporate his most recent rephrasing. Dr. Carson, if I don't agree to every general instruction she has used, calls me stubborn and insistent on my own way, while not paying very much attention at all to my rationale for attempting to do that particular effort in that way and ignoring what attempts I make to compromise, at least in her recent statements to me. Under the by-laws of the faculty of the Graduate School, one of the privileges, and I would like to emphasize that, of members is to serve as major professor for graduate students "working toward advanced degrees within the faculty member's field." Is it a privilege to work a student to distraction and sickness with frequent changes of mind, and in Dr. Carson's case, under-specificity, in Dr. Finn's case over-specificity? Certainly, the duties of a major professor, as implied in the University Handbook, are to work with the student to develop a study program and advise the unfolding of that program. It cannot be in the best interests, nor is it the responsibility or privilege of the faculty to command the style of a student, or at least, insist on imposing a specific style. That's the end of my statement at this time.

Dodd: Do you have anything further you want to add besides your written statement, Mr. Cant? At this point in time, I mean?
Cant: Not at this time, thank you.

Dodd: Okay. Before we proceed any further, I want to get it on the record, since you brought up—this is Reginald Dodd speaking—about how this matter came before the Board. That I first became aware of the—your appeal, Mr. Cant, on Monday, May the 12th, when the secretary gave me a message she had taken from you over the telephone, to the effect that you wanted to know when the Academic Hearing Board was going to meet. You needed to know what its decision was. I, at that point, tried to call the members of the committee and got in touch with only one of them. Later on that afternoon, I heard, through a third party, that Dean Strand was involved in this, and I called him. And he outlined, at that point, some of the matters being brought up here. However, I did not have, at that point, and did not get until yesterday, May 14th, when I went down myself and got it from Dean Strand, the copy of the letter in which you asked for a hearing, which you made through a third party, not directly to the Board. And I think I should point out, that it is not necessary that students go through a third party to get a hearing before the Board. All they have to do is come to the Chairman or any member of the Board and request it. And in any event, the Board could not convene a hearing until it got from the student involved, a complaint. I cannot convene in hearing on the basis of an approach by a third party. So when I got the complaint from Dean Strand yesterday, I immediately got in touch with the members of the committee.

Moon: (Eloquent Dodd, you 'did garbled no,' or diddle bang' in your 'blaring odd ed,' being 'a blind dodger' with 'blonde drag id.')

Dodd: In 3 days later, after I first found out about this matter, the Board has convened. So whatever else is involved, it is not a delay on the part of the Board. Professor Carson, are you ready to proceed?

Carson: Ja. Right.

Cant: Mr. Chairman, I brought my copies of my correspondence with Dean Strand; my two requests, per his instructions, are dated April 8th and April 15th. His request to you for a hearing is dated April 16th. That's a mont—

Dodd: Okay. Professor Carson.

Carson: I'm participating in this hearing with great reluctance. Let me say just a few personal things about Walter. I think he's a good student. He's done excellent work for me in the years that he's been here. He's done very fine scholarly papers, which I've given him 'A's on in every case. And I do believe that Walter Cant deserves his Masters, and as soon as this thesis, that he has before me and before others is in good enough shape, I'm willing to sign it but not in its present form. So that's the reason why I do this with great reluctance. I don't think anything is going to come out of this positively. This is just going to just cause more problems. I do want Walter to get his thesis. I think the material, the content of this, if it's in proper form, is acceptable to me. He knows what is necessary for signatures. Very very simple rules—in fact, they boil down to some very simple rules of English composition which is not arbitrary.

## The Thesis

Moon: (She certainly was a busty woman. Walter said they used to go running together, along with one of the other students. I wonder is she wears a holder for those things. I can't figure out what men see in oversized mammaries. Maybe Leigh I. Carson tames 'her logicians' with her 'il hag cronies' or 'aching oilers')

Carson: Students at this University learn to develop full paragraphs in essays, in theses, in first year—the freshman year. And what amazes me, is that Walter did display very good command of the language in his other papers but somehow, this thesis had to be different. Now, let me go back to the very beginning here. First of all, I don't consider 80 pages poetry the first draft of this thesis. We did not consider that part of the thesis at all. I consider the first draft, the 40 pages which Walter gave me last fall.

Cant: Mr. Chairman, may I interrupt Dr. Carson?

Dodd: Ah, well. We agreed that at the end of everybody's participation, you could make any rebuttals. I think it would be better and much— if Ms. Carson has no objections, I don't.

Carson: Professor Carson. I do have objections. I'd like to finish.

Dodd: OK, in that case, I think it would be best if we let him finish his presentation, and then you can bring up any points or cross-question him if you chose to—

Cant: (interrupts) Even though, I think I'm in the right according to Roberts' Rules, I will concede the point.

Dodd: Okay, Ms. Carson, will you proceed?

Carson: Yes. Professor Carson. Thank you. So the first draft—I want to get the chronicle of events down as best as I can recall them. The chronicle of events starts last fall, I believe. Isn't that true? When I got —

Cant: No, it isn't.

Carson: Last fall. When did I get these 40 pages?

Cant: The 40 pages last fall—

Carson (interrupts): Okay. All right—all right, that's where I'm beginning.

Moon: (I started doodling again. Taking apart names. I wonder if Professor Carson knows that one anagram of her name is 'girlish canoe'.)

Cant: (interrupts) The chronicle of events did not start—

Carson: (interrupts) Okay, that's where I'm beginning. I'm sorry. This is where I'm beginning. Walter is correct by saying that I was impressed with these 40 pages by and large. I thought they lent themselves to what in Philosophy is known as—well, at least I call it a Wittgensteinian format. I encouraged him to work up something along these lines. That's what I consider the first draft of this thesis. The second draft of the thesis is this 250 pages, which I did get in December. And, ah, do all of you have a copy of my comments? These are only about 1/2 the comments I made on these various drafts. Those who have, please follow along with these detailed comments. I don't consider these cursory, by the way. I think it stands at any intelligent mind looking at these, that I was not being cursory when I was making these comments.

Moon: (Leigh Carson, 'Scholar genii.' Much better. I heard Wittgenstein.)

Carson: —here are my general comments: I gave Walter a choice here. Either Wittgensteinian format or conventional thesis. The Wittgensteinian format is really an ideal. And I thought— I apologized to Walter afterwards, for it—encouraging him along this line, because once I saw the 250 page draft, I knew that this was not compatible in any way, absolutely no way, with the Wittgensteinian format that we were talking about. Let me explain a little bit about this Wittgensteinian format. Wittgenstein is a famous Austrian Philosopher, in English the linguistic traditions, who wrote a very famous philosophical book in 1922 called "Tractatus Logico-Philosophicus." It was numbered, aphoristic, pithy, very very profound, very very coherent series of philosophical statements. Okay? And I thought that some of the material in Walter's first draft lent itself to this format. And that is the reason why I gave him encouragement at that point. Now here, I'm saying about the Wittgensteinian format— It would require radical condensation in the entire manuscript, 250 pages, what I was talking about there, a radical condensation to maybe 50 or 60 pages, which is a normal length for a M.A. thesis, with elimination of most of the quotes.

Cant: (interrupts) Oh, may I add something? ah, Mr. Chairman—

Carson: (interrupts) I thought we had a rule for proceeding here.—

Cant: (interrupts) Please—

Moon: (Walter is making a mistake interrupting 'soaring chile')

Carson: Ah, Number two—

Dodd: (interrupts) Let's—Let him proceed.

Carson: Yeah. Number two—

Cant: (interrupts) No, Mr. Chairman. May I—May I please interrupt again? I will find difficulty in going back over these, and I think it would do the committee a disservice to have me attempt to reconstruct everything Dr. Carson said and try to correct it as it goes. or try to add simple things as we go along.

Carson: (interrupting) I think you've had a chance to reconstruct. It's my turn to reconstruct, ehr— events as I see them—

Dodd: (interrupts) Excuse me, Mr. Cant. Let me respond to it. Mr. Cant, we agreed to start with—that we would follow this procedure.

Moon: (With his 'bold gander id' he's a 'nod gerbil dad' and not a 'red goblin dad,' even when his wife said 'darling be odd.')

Cant: I'm sorry-

Dodd: So let's let him finish his presentation, and you can bring up any points you wish to when he finishes his presentation.

Cant: As you say.

Carson: Okay. I—if Walter were to continue with this Wittgensteinian format—Already at this point, and I submit as evidence something at which

## The Thesis

Walter claims to be a late comment. This is a fairly early one. Here is the comment on the last page of this thing. 'I regret now format, because the draft, (the 250 page draft) that I encouraged you to the Wittgensteinian certainly doesn't fit it. It must be concise, to the point, with an absolute minimum of extraneous material.' This 250-page draft had fantastic extraneous material. Like I told him one time, there were ten to twelve different theses going on at the same time. This is not compatible with the Wittgensteinian format. This draft is the antithesis of this, the Wittgensteinian format'—So on. That was an early comment not a late comment. So that was my choice—that was the option for Walter. Either condense this thing radically and get back to the original idea or do a conventional thesis. Now my specific comments, which I submit again were not cursory at all, but I spent many hours over this thesis. Let me just point out some—ah, page 4 and 5—'long quotes,' that is 1/2 page quotes. Inexcusable in either format. 'Full caps there—the original draft (the 40 pages which I was impressed with)—the original draft seemed to have things more organized than this one,' which was totally unorganized. I was being generous there. It was extremely diffuse. 'Extraneous material all over the place.' 'A simple, concise thesis of three parts: being, language, and philosophy.' He had 14 chapters in that 250 page thesis. Page 8—'too many quotes-we want Cant'—I didn't want a list of quotes. This 250 page draft seemed like a list of his notes that he took reading the books. That's fine, but that didn't even serve as a draft to the thesis. The whole tenor of these comments are almost always virtually negative. I've found some very good—ah, the thesis still contained some of the kernel material which I was impressed with. Some of the rather aphoristic statements about the body, which I think are very good, and they would remain in the thesis. What Walter did was pile extraneous material upon extraneous material upon extraneous material on this fairly acceptable first draft of 40 pages. Notice this quote here on page 10—'Attempt to answer your rhetorical questions.' That draft was filled with rhetorical questions that were never answered. —'it seems like you definitely have more of a conventional thesis going here. The process then would be cut and to elaborate in the old-fashioned way.' Like you've done so well in your other papers. Walter's trying to do too much, too many topics, too much attention to the whole of everything.

Moon: Pardon me, wasn't his thesis on the whole of Being? You know, that reminds me, Cornelius Ford, the cousin of Dr. Johnson, told him to 'study the principles of everything' to ensure that an acquaintance with life would precede his inquiries into life. He suggested that he shake the trunk to move all the branches. After all it is the trunk that branches out and not the twigs that trunk down. Furthermore, Wittgenstein meant his proposition to cover everything scientific, leaving out only ethics, I think.

Carson: OK. OK. Where was I? Yes. The tenor of my remarks are definitely against used the Wittgensteinian format, because I'm quite convinced at this point that Walter can't handle it. Wittgenstein handled it. I'm sorry to say, Walter Cant did not handle it. 'One sentence paragraphs'. Okay, I hammered away at this for months, and you can look— I'll send around examples of what I mean by—'One sentence paragraphs, long quotes not commented on.' Long quotes are fine in a thesis as long as you comment on them and try to draw material out of them. Walter just stated these quotes down on the thesis. 'One sentence paragraph. Okay for the Wittgensteinian format if they're pithy enough.' That's the whole genius of this way of approaching Philosophy. if you can write a one sentence paragraph that ways what needs to be said, that's fine. Walter Cant was not doing that in this thesis.

Cant: (interrupts) Dr. Carson, would you kindly point out that you're passing around the 4th draft and not the 7th draft—Much less the *lebensform* draft.

Carson: Listen, I don't want to get into this. This is— I'm talking about the 2nd draft.

Cant: (interrupts) No, Dr. Carson, I made the designations and I insist that they be held to—

Carson: Chairman, Mr. Chairman, would you—we're following certain rules here.

Dodd: (interrupting) Mr. Cant, would you please refrain from interjecting comments until he gets through with his presentation.

Carson: Yes, I just explained—

Cant: I believe— Mr. Chairman, I believe made the point that in this meeting if we could do it this way we could—we would, but I object strongly to Dr. Carson's errors or extraneous information that bears no relevance to this meeting.

Dodd: Mr. Cant, Dr. Carson did not interrupt you in your presentation and I would appreciate it if you would extend him the same courtesy.

Cant: The circumstances are slightly different, Mr. Chairman. Dr. Carson is not on trial.

Dodd: Well, neither are you. This is not a legal proceeding.

Cant: It was not used as a legal term.

Dodd: Well—I—I don't see where we're getting anywhere with this—Just let him continue —

Carson: I would like to continue here. I— I think this material—May I have a ruling of the hearing board whether or not this material is relevant or not—that I'm speaking to right here?

Dodd: I assume it is—Some of this is over my head.

Moon: (That's not all it's over, Dodd, you 'dear blind dog,' your 'dog brand lied' You think you 'dig olden bard,' but sound more like an 'inbred dog lad' and look like a 'ribald dog end.')

Carson: (interrupts) Is—Are there—Are there any objections from the board about the relevance of this material that I'm presenting?

Dodd: I have none.

Sooner: Sooner is speaking. I have none. I presume anything Mr. Cant can explain and his turn is coming—if it turns out that this is irrelevant, he'll explain that to us and we'll find that out.

Holland: Holland speaking. I agree with the Chairman.

Moon: (Mars Holland had the rough hands of a farmer, the red checkered shirt of a farmer, and the weak dripping nose of a hippie, 'mr nasal hold' drifts down 'random halls,' thinking 'darn all homs,' or maybe he should 'lash norm lad,' but after all, a 'nod harms all.'

O'dell: O'dell, I agree.

Moon: (I was waiting for her to bring us cookies and milk. I forgot that housewives can be professors as well, if they teach home ec. Professor Lisa was short and rotund, with a face like Liz Taylor and hair like a Liz Taylor wig. Lisa O'dell, just 'ladle lois,' an 'aisle doll' in whose head an 'idea lolls.' Maybe the 'ill old sea' was one of the 'old allies' with the rest of the board.)

Cant: (interrupts) Mr. Chairman, I would—I would agree to be silent if, if Dr. Carson insists—

Carson: (interrupts) You have already agreed to be silent.

Cant: Please be quiet, Dr. Carson. if Dr. Carson insists on presenting drafts, parts of different drafts, then I will be silent if this committee agrees to read every draft of that thesis for comparative purposes.

Dodd: Ah, Mr. Cant, since we're not getting anywhere, I'll make a ruling that Mr. Carson will proceed with her presentation, and when she gets through, you can bring up any points you wish to. You can challenge anything she says. But until she gets through with her presentation, I request that you remain silent.

Carson: Okay, I have sent around samples of this—this is the 3rd or 4th draft. Okay, yeah, I agree, I'm sorry, that particular draft is a typed draft, so it must be the 4th. Okay, but it was not much better than this 2nd draft, which I'm referring to now. Many of the comments that I made were not heeded. Some—another thing that I might as well start passing around—here is a sample of about 20, 25 pages where I say, 'cut, keep, or elaborate C K E R,' and I hope you notice the profusion of cuts in this thesis. Okay, turn to the second page here, the handwritten material. 'This needs a lot more work before okayed by committee. Still lacks coherence. Too many quotes. Not enough straight-forward commentary on the quotes. Too poetic, not straight-forward conventional thesis we need.' 'Okay, at this point, I was absolutely sure that the Wittgensteinian format was not viable at all. My suggestion, again, 'Begin with the pre-Socratics, Aristotle'—so forth. Draw out the views, poetry, philosophy. Very pedestrian, very straight-forward, the M.A. thesis is complete. Another thing that was eliminated from here was a suggestion along 3rd or 4th draft, that Walter cut down to the introduction held written, the first chapter, and to retain the tenth to the fourteenth chapters. This advice was not taken. I found 14 chapters in an

M.A. thesis absolutely too, too much material. He had 10 or 12 different things going on here.

One of the things about a Master's thesis, by the way, that it has a specific topic that one keeps to. Each one of these chapters, these 14 chapters was a virtually,—a different thesis topic. I don't think I was being arbitrary or eccentric or out of hand by advising Walter to specify, to be more specific, to develop these one sentence paragraphs, so that they made sense—a rule, basic English composition. You don't leave a one sentence just hanging without any sort of transition or coherence to it or development. That's what I was taught in English composition. Develop your thoughts. These thoughts were not developed. Okay. On the third page here, these are comments that I made on the last draft that I saw. And I'm not going to quibble about how many drafts. I think there's extreme draft inflation in Walter's account of what's going on here.

Let me point out something to you here. On the first page of the letter to Dean Strand in the second full paragraph. Let me just read through this and show you the inconsistency in the chronicle of events as Walter sees them. 'in October, I wrote an 80 page poetic statement of the thesis which no one wanted to read or did.' I don't consider that the first draft. 'In November, I rewrote it in 40 pages of prose. Professor Carson read it and was so impressed that she wrote me a note urging the next draft to be done in the Wittgensteinian format, numbered aphorisms, or lebensforms.' That-really doesn't apply there. 'In December, I enlarged that, 3rd draft (I call that the 2nd draft—to 250 pages—I call that the 2nd draft.) which Dr. Finn and Mr. Kraft refused to or would not read—while Dr. Carson wrote the note.' I would submit that what I wrote here was not a note but there was another full page of single spaced, typewritten comments on this—this second draft, as I call it. It said that I 'had scanned it.' I submit that I wasn't scanning, but I was taking very careful and meticulous note of what was going on here. 'Found it to be true prosaic.'

Well look at my comments. I think I said a lot more than that. 'I chose, (Now that's the 2nd draft as I call it—okay, as I stipulated) I chose to continue in the mode of the Wittgensteinian for the 5th draft.' But what happened to the 3rd draft, the 4th draft? There's a little bit of draft inflation involved in this paragraph here, okay. Now this is the final draft as I was reading it in early April. And this was a draft that was presumably going to a typist. And I was just scandalized on every page, at the presumption on Walter's part that a typist could actually follow what he was doing here. So what I was doing here, was doing some very technical pedestrian things about—what about a reference here? What about punctuation here? what book? Make clear for typist. Do not use contractions. Mark the chapters.' How's a typist going to write— type a thesis if the chapters aren't marked? 'Fix up footnote references.' This must be clean for the typist, otherwise you'll be wasting money. Very confusing for the typist and the disjunctive 'set of quotes. 'Delete or compress.' Fourth paragraph—Very close paraphrase of my—my own work, by the way.

## The Thesis

That's another thing I objected to. Almost lifted right out of my own articles. 'Still don't like these short undeveloped paragraphs.'

Cant: That's wrong, Leigh, and you know it.
Dodd: I won't say it again.
Carson: May I continue? Now this is the final draft that Walter wants final done in early April to meet the deadline. 'I think I'm ready to sign this after I talk to Sam and Ronn.' Then I made my qualifications. 'Still too many issues going on here. Too many theses going on. Paragraphs not well developed. Still too many long quotes that have no commentary on the.' Okay? I was trying to do the best I could to get Walter out of here. I wanted him to get the thesis. In fact, maybe I was too generous here, but I was extremely scandalized by the presumption on his part, that a typist could even make a clean copy of what he gave me. Punctuation at the end of the page. Is this a clean copy for a typist to type? Disjunctive paragraphs marked in blue. Short developed paragraphs.

Now one of the things that I was looking for in this final draft was some revisions. But what I got, and I could see where the revisions were made because it was either in blue or black ink. I was desperately looking for the blue or the black. What I saw were just clip quotes from previous drafts pasted on top of one another, making it even more confusing, more diffuse, and more disjunctive. Please sort of emphasize, empathize I mean, with my situation here as a thesis advisor. I think I was bending over backwards trying to help Walter here. 'Lacking names for some of these references.' A typist was going to type this for a final rough draft to be approved. These arrows will really confuse the typist. Again 'short choppy paragraphs.' Are these really paragraphs? 'Inexcusably long quote.' Top: 'Full references for your typist. Underline all titles. (That's handy for a final draft.) Underline book titles. (That's simple English composition.) maddening disjunctiveness here and elsewhere.' Do these sound like positive comments for someone to sign? I think I was really sort of being— I was really compromising myself, when I state, I think I'm ready to sign this. Is it clear from my comments here that I was really ready to sign this? No. 'Rather enigmatic sections here.' I—I'm asking for very very simple things here. Like—basic rules of English composition, which are not arbitrary at all, but standard for any thesis form. It was standard for Ludwig Wittgenstein, when he was doing his famous work. He made his references and he punctuated clearly.

Cant: Excuse me, Leigh, but Wittgenstein didn't use references. There are no quotes or sources in the Tractatus. He was so obsessed with being original that he did not acknowledge his intellectual debts much at all.

Carson: No!

Cant: Yes, he uses a lot of Schopenhauer's stuff, metaphors and ideas. He also—

Carson: No! Who says? What?

Cant: Ayer says, for one. Thought maybe Wittgenstein wanted to project his philosophy *ab initio*. Furthermore, Wittgenstein based some of his ideas on Kant; for instance, where Kant thought metaphysicians were confused dreamers, Wittgenstein said that all philosophers were babblers of nonsense.

Moon: (Hear, hear. One of his biographers said that Kant's life was like the most regular of regular verbs; the people of Konigsberg set their watches by his afternoon walks. Kant had been educated by polymaths, scholars in many fields, but he emerged in Prussian society and became a card-playing, elegant gossip. I wondered if Walter would end up like his phonetic namesake.)

Dodd: Mmmm.

Carson: You might be right. But, that isn't important here. We don't need more of your almost namesake.

Cant: Actually, he is my namesake. Both of our ancestors came from Scotland in the, uhmm, 1600s, fleeing puritans I think, only they changed their name from Cant.

Carson: Okay, I've already referred to this. 'I think I'm ready to sign this after I talk to Sam and Ronn.' I did talk to Sam and Ronn. Both of them were not willing to sign it. With all of my reservations I wasn't about to try to convince them to sign it. This is just a complete misrepresentation of what happened here. At no time, did I try to convince Dr. Kraft to sign this. We all agreed that it needed more work. Unfortunately, I was very very sad about this. Cause Walter had worked very very hard. He lives in my basement. I know how much work he put into this, but I was scandalized at this final draft. It was patchwork, and—and this is untypical of Walter because I'd read his other papers at the graduate level. I was very pleased with them. And this was very very untypical. I just couldn't believe it. Draft after draft. It got worse instead of better. more disjunctive. I wanted some very thorough revision and rewriting. I never found that. I never asked Walter to alter the style repeatedly. I was just asking for some very basic rules of English composition. Well developed paragraphs, a long—long quotations are okay if you comment on them. Coherence, transition—basic—this is what I call style, in which I think it's significant. This is not style in the sense of, you know, your phrasing is a little off. No, this is basic, fundamental English composition, that I was having trouble with. 'No transition between paragraphs, incoherent, uncommented long quotes.'—so forth. I, I think I made my point.

Dodd: Excuse me, does that mean your finished with your presentation?
Carson: Yes.
Dodd: Okay.—Mr. Cant, if—is there anything you want to bring up, ask him for clarification—challenge?
Cant: Yes sir, many things.
Dodd: Go ahead then.
Cant: Unfortunately, I can't read my writing. First of all, I think we ought to get the most obvious thing out of the way. Let us refer to that letter to the Dean

again. I don't like faulting Professor Carson on her ability to read, but she has—

Dodd: Which letter are you referring to, Mr. Cant?

Cant: I'm referring to the first letter to Dean Strand.

Dodd: Oh, Okay, the 7th of April, right?

Cant: The 2nd draft—that's the 2nd paragraph. Okay, according to this letter, the 1st draft was mentioned in the first paragraph. The 2nd draft is mentioned in the first sentence of the 2nd paragraph. The 3rd draft is mentioned in the words, 'in November, I rewrote it in 40 pages of prose.' That is the 3rd draft. Professor Carson read it and was so impressed, that she wrote me a note urging the next draft to be done in Wittgensteinian format which, are as Wittgenstein suggested, lebensforms, living forms. In December, I enlarged that 3rd draft to 250 pages. That is the 4th draft, and not as Dr. Carson tried to understand, the 2nd draft. After that 4th draft, Dr. Carson suggested that I make it more brief and enigmatic or more prosaic. I chose to continue in the mode of Wittgenstein for the 5th draft. That is the 5th draft. In February, I did a 6th draft, and in March, I finished the 7th draft. The point that I want to make, also, is that there are a thousand pages of it.

And I would also like to mention a few other things that Dr. Carson left out. For instance, Wittgenstein's final piece, I believe was, what, 150 pages long, whereas mine is 170. I believe his original draft was somewhere around 700 or 800, but he had a better editor than I have, and one further thing about Wittgenstein, I believe it was quite a number of years before he got his Masters or his Doctorate, or his Degree, shall I say. Apparently, if I don't follow him in one sense, I follow him in the other. Secondly, Dr. Carson mentions long quotes. That's true. I did have some long quotes in the thesis, and the reason I put them in was because, simply, that there were people like Wittgenstein or Merleau Ponty, who believe it or not, could say lots of things a lot better than I could, and it seemed ridiculous to me to paraphrase Wittgenstein and Merleau Ponty, just to satisfy the template Dr. Carson used in her thesis, which I have here, as well as every thesis written in the past 30 years for the Idaho Modern Philosophy Department, and I maintain there's an average of 5 quotes per page in those theses, whereas mine only averaged 1 1/2. You'd have to read everything that I have in order to confirm those statistics, however. I also read through Dr. Carson's last graduate student, who, believe it or not, had a quote that lasted 2 1/2 pages without very much elucidation, but then Dr. Carson and I disagreed on that as well.

Secondly, ah, oh gee, I've already been over it three times, haven't I? I guess I should go on. Furthermore, Professor Carson faults my one sentence paragraphs. That's resulted from a misunderstanding when I wrote the 3rd draft. You see, I wasn't sure of myself, and so I wrote each sentence as a separate unit so that it could be replaced if it was incorrect, which is where Dr. Carson got the idea of putting it in the lebensform format and suggested that I try that. Each paragraph was marked by an indention. I have written several notes to Dr. Carson and Dr.

Finn explaining why the sentences are like that, and the fact that they are not one sentence paragraphs, and since we're going to befuddle the whole issue before us, I might as well be as guilty as the rest. I would like to read a note that I wrote to Professor Finn in March: "The sentences are indented for ease of correction. They are not paragraphs, Leigh always forgets." Many of the quoted were not identified since I didn't want to do the bibliographic work until it was approved. Chapter 10 is ...

Moon: (I tuned everyone out for a while. Walter was going on answering the Chairman of the department point by point. I was thinking about the new secretary in the library. What a dish. But too shy. She only likes to talk about Nabokov, so I'm going to have to read—I wonder if Thor? Nah, too traditional, although I thought men fantasized about having two women at once. Too dangerous here at Ida-ho-hum anyway.)

Cant: ... have an outline of the thesis, which has been standard since last October. I'll pass it around if you like, along with some of Dr. Carson's remarks, some of which she left out. So, you see, the thesis was very well-planned. I followed the outline scrupulously, when I laid out my notes and when I made Leigh's changes. I'm passing around a page from the 6th and 7th drafts to show you that I did, indeed, make the requested changes.

I regret—I'm flattered, first of all that you will read some of my thesis. Naturally, I'm disappointed that you didn't get to read the best parts, and I hope you haven't been unduly biased by the fact that each sentence seems to be a separate unit. They are not separate paragraphs because I'm following the rules of composition and each one is not a separate thought. The sentences do go together in an organic way.

Moon: Perhaps if you told everyone what distinguishes a paragraph.

Cant: Of course, yes, the paragraph mark, right there in the margin. Well, I won't pass around any more of the drafts because I don't believe the committee wants to, or is qualified, or even has any business judging whether I know as much of Merleau-Ponty as Professor Carson thinks. ...

Moon: (I had actually read some of this M-P, who had said that "The philosophy placed in books has ceased to challenge men." Apparently the punctuation still challenges them. More about the sentences and the drafts and the punctuation. I could scream. That reminds me of the new girl at the Circulation Desk—what a perfect description, circulation—Sandra. I should see if she wants to go swimming or play racquetball . . . hmmm)

Cant: Professor Carson's, to use his own term "scandalous interpretation," of my paraphrasing of his own articles. If you would please look at this page from the 4th draft, you will notice that his article was quoted and attributed to him and Professor Carson wrote a note in the margin saying "You do not need to quote your major professor. I do not need that honor. Just paraphrase it." Now, please notice that it does not appear in the 7th draft, because I didn't feel that

## The Thesis

I could paraphrase it as well as he said it, so I cut it; then, used a quote from Heidegger, if I remember. ...

Moon: (more on the tale of the typists, all 6 or—I don't think anyone is ever going to look at any of this stuff. It will always be just Walter's word versus theirs, regardless of the facts. I asked him why he didn't just bail out and go study somewhere reputable. He said that was what he'd done the time before, and his girlfriend told him to stay and fight for it. She's nice looking, too. I wonder if they're close ...)

Cant: ... some of the drafts have gone through five or six revisions. Naturally I was alarmed when the questions never stopped. No matter how many pieces Leigh shows you of old drafts, those were not the one ready to type for the final thesis. By the way, I corrected my own mistakes, had to, because Professor Carson was so intent of finding one-sentence paragraphs that she overlooked any errors. She's admitted to me and others that there are no giant conceptual errors.

Personally, I am not thrilled with the direction my thesis has taken. I'd hoped to do it in poetic form because of the subject matter; this has been argued by M-P and Heidegger, that metaphysics requires a certain kind of approach, and since Heidegger has written chapters of his books in poetic form, it seemed—

Carson: I think *not*. I've studied Heidegger and in the *Sein and Zeit*—

Cant: I think *so*. For Heidegger, poetry is the most powerful of arts; he states that "All art ... is ... essentially poetry." Merleau-Ponty, with a few differences, praises literature for displaying the full force of significance of an age of thought.

Carson: How do you think poetry presents Being more than mathematics or prose or art. Look at your quote from Rilke. It is not linked anywhere to anything.

Cant: Let's read it then, in part: "Center, how you draw yourself /out of all things, regaining yourself/even from things in flight ..." As I do in the thesis, the poem is related to gravity and centeredness, to Being and beings, to the psychological and the physical. In a way that mere prose cannot connect or even suggest. Even Wittgenstein thought poetry was the only way that—

Carson: No! I've studied Wittgenstein. He never said—

Cant: I do remember the quote, from one of his notebooks, "I think I summed up my attitude to philosophy when I said: philosophy ought really to be written only as a poetic composition." In the quote he was revealing himself as someone who cannot quite do what he would like to be able to do. I took that to mean—

Carson: I'll have to see it in writing.

Cant: Of course, the reference is on the draft. Where was I? Oh, it seemed to me that I might make a good attempt in mine to describe the nature of being-as-being. I don't want to drivel on about the subject matter of the thesis. I'm just unhappy with Professor Carson's attitude toward it. She claims that she's done a lot of work, and maybe in the 2nd draft she did, but each subsequent draft she's done less and less, because she's been laboring under the belief that she's read it all before. She's said she's looked for black and blue ink, without realizing that I retyped many of the changes. Because they were typewritten, there's no way she could ascertain changes unless she did read the whole thing again, which she's admitted not doing. If you look at her comments, again, you'll see "cut," "elaborate"—general comments over and over. I wish you could read the difference between the last two drafts—or any two—because I did cut and elaborate, although not always the same order that Dr. Carson desired. So I think it's just—it's unfortunate that we've had to confine our discussion to this and not whether style is a reason to refuse a thesis, or to okay it, and then change your mind because two of the committee members who did not read very much at all were able to convince you. Oh—There's just one more parenthetical statement I would like to make. I asked Dr. Carson to try to convince Dr. Finn to sign it since Dr. Finn had promised to sign it if Dr. Carson had signed it, his reasons being that he had not read it, and I believe this is standard operating procedure for the department. I don't know how well Dr. Finn has read other theses for which he was not major professor, but I don't—I think Dr. Carson's misinterpreted my statements. Most of my statements about Dr. Carson are bad enough without her adding more to them. That's all I have to say in reply to the— to Professor Carson.

 Carson: Mr. Chairman, I have some brief remarks before Dr. Finn continues.

 Dodd: Yeah, go ahead, Leigh.

 Carson: I—I'd like to refer again to page 1 2 3, 4 of these comments that I made. By the way, these are only about half of the comments I made on the series—let me—Let me first admit that I was getting very very tired of getting—of this every time, when I was expecting a thesis of 60 to 100 pages. I—I have my limits of reading. Yes, I skimmed over a lot of the stuff in the 4th and 5th and 6th or how many drafts that Walter wants to—and I noticed upon that skimming, surprisingly many of the same stuff rearranged, this sort of thing—and Walter claims that my comments are general on that last draft in April. Read through these please. They're very very specific. Most of them are just merely technical things that I hoped I didn't have to worry about. This is what I m mean by being scandalized. This was supposed to go to a typist. He was ready—He had one ready to type—a final draft. And I could—I couldn't believe that Walter expected a typist to type this as a final rough draft of a thesis. These are not general comments, but the they're very very specific. Specific references to his format there.

 Cant: Who—Mr. Chairman, I —

 Carson: (interrupts) Walter, I have the floor.—

 Cant: Excuse me.—Wittgenstein also said: "Each of the sentences I write is trying to say the whole thing, i.e., the same thing over and over again; it as though they were all simply views of one object seen from different angles." Don't forget this whole thesis thing was a phenomenological spiral—

 Carson: —I'm very very sorry but—

Cant: Yes, of-course. I didn't realize you still had the floor. Please accept my apologies to your committee.

Carson:—one full page there, that at no time—Walter presumes to know what happened on the telephone between Ronn Kraft and I, and on the telephone between Caesar Sam Finn and me. He presumes to tell us what happened there. At no time, and I wish I would get these gentlemen's confirmation on this, did I try to convince them to sign this thing. We were bemoaning the fact that the draft was not ready. And it wouldn't take too many minutes for either Ronn Kraft or Sam Finn to see that this manuscript was not ready to—for typing. You wouldn't have to spend two—two hours reading through it to see whether or not it was ready.

Dodd: Is that?—

Carson: These long quotes thing again—What I was most upset about using the long quotes, and—and long quotes that just orient after one another, was that there was virtually no commentary on them. Like he said, he wanted to let the—the authors speak their say. Still, I think in any sort of conventional thesis—now remember again, I thought the Wittgensteinian format would not go. I would not sign it. I didn't think it was a viable option. That Walter kept on thinking that he was right in a Wittgensteinian thesis, and I kept discouraging him in this—direction. The long quotes did not have sufficient commentary, did not really fit the thrust of what he was trying to say. They were very diffuse and very misleading.

Finn: My turn?

Dodd: Just a minute Sam. Are you—

Carson: Yeah, I think that's—

Cant: (interrupts) May I make a response?

Dodd: Yeah, you want to go ahead? (to Finn)

Cant:—to his response of the responses of the responses.

Dodd: Yes, go ahead.

Cant: Excellent. Thank you. I confess, the reason I want to make a response is simply a desire in part to the last word. I will repeat once again— I did—Dr. Carson promised me that he would attempt to persuade Dr. Finn. He said, 'I am going to call Dr. Finn and Dr. Kraft and see if I can persuade them.' Those were approximately the words he—

Carson (interrupting): I'm glad I didn't write any such thing like that down on paper.

Cant: I'm glad you didn't to—I mean you could—evidence standing out—

Carson: (laughing) Yeah—Cause I think that's a lie, Walter. Quite frankly—

Cant: Well, um— I never presumed to know what was spoken between you, just how it ended up.

Carson: I'm sorry.

Moon: (Carson should be sorry. Her name letters also spell 'echoing liars.')

Dodd: Well, ah, let's—proceed—

Cant: Also I would like—oh, by the way Leigh, I had the floor—

Carson: I'm sorry, I couldn't restrain myself—

Cant: Yes, you're excused. Meanwhile, I wish the committee would only examine the 7th draft, since that was the one approved.

Dodd: Well, let's do—restrain ourselves.

Cant: I'm sorry Mr. Chairman. It's difficult, because I spent a lot of time, and I have more invested in this than Dr. Finn or Dr. Carson. And I think a lot of Dr. Carson's comments today are brought by the fact, I—I called the committee to challenge her judgment, which I can understand she and Dr. Finn do not like. But I think that—that Dr. Carson's comments as a whole were simply either too general or too specific. For instance, I would like to point out that after she had read the entire thesis in two hours on that Monday night, and given it to me that Tuesday morning, I had made these corrections within the two hours. I had—let me— let's go through specific corrections. 'What book?'—on page 7 in the introduction. I believe I put a comma and said 'in the Metaphysics.' Each of these comments I went through. If there were—for instance—under the comment 10.5, 'these arrows will readily confuse the typist.' I did go through and I cut it, and I believe that if anyone who would refer to the draft—or anyone who would refer to the draft would find that these corrections were made, and I contend that they were made even before Dr. Carson even talked to Dr. Finn.

They were certainly going to be made before the Typist. Once again, if Dr. Carson insists that they're problems in English composition I must insist that instead of having on my committee two Philosophers and an Art Theorist, that we simply have three English professors to decide whether or not this thesis is worthy of English Composition 1. I—I apologize for going on and on, Mr. Chairman—

Carson: I would like to make two short comments and then—First of all, about the short paragraphs—

Cant: (laughs in amusement)

Carson: This is really an incredible thing. So they are just notes that hopefully and miraculously will follow—fall into a coherent paragraph. I—I'm just completely amazed at the presumption in that sort of theory. I—I'm quite willing in this last draft to have all of that just one paragraph. That—It still is very very confusing. That by marking arbitrarily—Here's a paragraph, and then halfway down the page another paragraph—This is not going to perform any miracle about coherence and disjunctiveness. Those problems are still going to remain. And I—I'm perfectly willing to have any third person, party from the English Department to look at the—some of these that I marked and to confer in private, whether or not these meet basic rules for composition and intelligibility, coherence transition, and proper paragraph development. I'm quite willing to let a third party look at this.

Dodd: With your approval or consent Sam, there's a couple of things I'd like

# The Thesis

to get clear before we go to you. is that all right? Okay. This is Reginald Dodd. Leigh, let me ask you and then we'll see if Mr. Cant, agrees, but it's not clear in my mind. At what point in all these drafts that you suggested to Mr. Cant that he give up this Wittgensteinian format and go to the more orthodox way.

Carson: Right. As far as my numbering of drafts go—it is—he gave me 40 pages which I was impressed with. He expanded that to 250. At that point, I give him a choice, as you ca see in my comments here. At that point, I'm very discouraged and very pessimistic about whether he can fulfill this Wittgensteinian ideal at all. Really what I wanted was a conventional thesis here and this is what this 250 page thing essentially was.

Dodd: That's the one that Mr. Cant refers to as his 3rd draft.

Carson: Yeah. Yeah, 4th draft or 3rd draft, I suppose.

Cant: 4th.

Dodd: Okay—

Carson: And let me just refer again to the comments on the last page of my comments here 'I regret now that I encouraged you on the Wittgensteinian format because the draft certainly doesn't fit it. it must be concise, to the point, with an absolute minimum of extraneous material.' This draft, either the 2nd or 3rd, whatever you call it, very early on, this would be December last year—'This draft is the antithesis of this'—that is the Wittgensteinian format. I was definitely discouraging Walter from trying to beat his head against a wall in something that wasn't going to come to fruition.

Dodd: Okay, well, that clears that up. Now I have—

Cant: Oh, pardon me Mr. Chairman. It does not clear it up. Actually, I would like to point out is that that 250 page draft was followed by one that was 145 pages. I would like—although it's, of course, not the jurisdiction of this committee—but I would like to point out that somewhere 105 pages were cut. If I remember correctly, four entire chapters were cut, and at least half of what Dr. Carson suggested was cut out. And I don't think Dr. Carson's one-sided presentation will help any committee to decide.

Dodd: Okay, there was one other matter I wanted to—ah, this example that you passed around here numbered 177 to 196—

Carson: Yeah.

Dodd: Do you know what draft this is?

Carson: That's—yeah, that's the one I was trying to approve in April, catching Mr. Cant up.

Dodd: This year—

Carson: Yes, this year it went over 200 pages.

Dodd: In April of— this is the—

Cant: 186.

Carson: That was the draft in April that I was correcting for the final. It was over 200—

Cant: Oh.—Mr. Chairman —I—I believe Professor Carson is mistaken. If I may see that, I would be happy to identify the number of draft—

Dodd: Here it is.

Cant: May I also say that that draft which Dr. Carson said she would approve is in my possession, and it was typed by Dr. Finn's secretaries, and that draft came to 186 pages if you would like to examine the entire draft. This is from the 4th draft, the 250 page one, and these chapters here were cut in entirety after, I believe page 188. That is to say that pages 189-250 did not exist in the 5th draft. I wish Dr. Carson would remember which notebook she got examples on my thesis for before she presents them to the committee—

Carson: (interrupts) I'm sorry. I'm very confused about these drafts. I still think it's—

Cant: I wish—I wish Dr. Carson would —

Carson: —fantastically long and unwieldy thesis that I was not willing to sign.

Cant: I would like to ask the committee, That if the committee will not be confused, I would admit that possibly I have inflated a number of drafts by including that one poetic draft which I did for my own benefit, knowing that no one would accept it. The reason—but since I've already inflated it and made the designation, I would like everyone to refer to each draft as it has been numbered in the letter and on the drafts themselves —- if possible.

Dodd: Well ah—I would appreciate it— seeing a later draft and—or at least part of it, some examples, since these were—

Cant: Mr.—Dr. Carson has—

Carson: I have the latest draft right here. Here is 81 pages—

B Dodd: I don't have to do it right now. I can do this later after the hearing—

Carson: It's about—It's about 170 or 180 pages.

Cant: Exactly.

Dodd: But I would like to have one of the later drafts—after—

Carson: This is it.

Dodd: —to look at at this stage of the hearing. Okay, I—That's all I had to—Any other member of the committee have any questions they would like to direct either at Ms. Carson or Mr. Cant? Yeah, go ahead —

Carson: Professor Carson.

Moon: Can I ask a proper last question of Ms. Leigh? I mean I don't know whether— (I sympathized with her always being called Ms., or 'miss lay' but not with her worse treatment of Cant.)

Dodd: Go ahead.

Moon: In your year's of advising students in the Philosophy program would it not be an unusual Master's candidate that would be capable of undertaking a paper on an advanced level according to the Wittgensteinian format? I mean I'm— I'm only saying that as one that has been around the Tractatus a couple of times and found it challenging—that they would be a rather unique student.

# The Thesis

Carson: It would.—yeah, right. And given Walter's propensities in poetry and creative writing, this would have made a beautiful thesis in creative writing—I was willing to encourage him, at that point to see what he could do.

Moon: I—Very well. You encouraged him. (With all these I, I, I's, testimony was sounding like a Mexican dance.)

Carson: I was very very dissatisfied. Okay, now somebody may say that I—that was a piece of bad judgment on my part. I was trying to—I was trying to give in to Walter's desire to do a rather poetic thesis, and—I let him know that that 250 page draft—it wasn't what I had in mind as far as a Wittgensteinian format. maybe I was wrong in encouraging him at that point. I do contend that after I saw this huge opus in his many drafts, I knew that Walter was not disciplined enough to tackle what in what we've termed as the Wittgensteinian format.

Dodd: Does anybody else have any questions to address to —

Sooner: No— I want to find out what draft this comes from—is it 40 pages—40 that 55—

Cant: Sir, I believe that's also the 4th draft. I was watching Dr. Carson, and again she passed around various parts of the 4th draft—-

Dodd: These come from the same draft—

Cant: I would—I would hope that we just pass around parts of each draft simultaneously—

Sooner: Yeah—

Cant: —Due to the fact that the pages are numbered and not according to draft—

Sooner: I'll buy that.

Cant: In other words, there are probably at least, at least four pages marked 100 here somewhere.

Sooner: Yeah, I'd like to see those also—

Dodd: Leigh, do these —

Sooner: Something of the more recent one.

Dodd: Do these—They're not numbered consecutively, but do you know if they came from the same draft, Leigh? These two different particles—

Carson: Yes, I—they did come from the same draft.

Sooner:—right date of the draft —

Carson: Here's some beautiful sort of a beautiful example of what I call arbitrary paragraphing

Dodd: Well, um, Leigh—

Carson: Just take a look for yourself.

Dodd: Let's hold up with circulating of these things—cause really for—if we're going to make anything of this, they're going to have to be identified in some kind of a sequence.

Cant: Yes. Mr. Chairman, I would like to suggest that we don't ever pay any attention to them because obviously unless this committee is willing to devote as much time as Dr. Carson has in ten months, which is to say at least ten hours, nothing is going to get done. Because the drafts are not at issue. The problem is not whether I'm disciplined enough to handle lebensform. The problem is simply that I have attempted to follow Dr. Carson's instructions and write in prose for the final three drafts. And the fact is that Dr. Carson approved it, and now I want someone to recognize that.

Dodd: Well, ah, the reason I brought this up is because, I've seen this and I wanted to find out at what stage it was put in, and I'm concerned with the relative aspects of it and not the—

Cant: Yes sir, I can see that. I—I would be happy if we could take the same section from all seven drafts and you could understand how it's—how it's changed from prose to poetry to lebensform to lebensform to prose, prose, prose, and how many things have been changed—

Moon: I must have dozed off—

Dodd: Well, I think we have heard enough, and we have certainly seen enough paper. The Board thanks the Committee for its patience and Ellsin Moon from the Library. We have enough to deliberate, and we shall make as decision in a timely manner. Good day.

You may turn off the recorder, now. Thank you.

Cant with Snakeman (acryllic on glass)

## 6 *Really Living, Going Running*

I had a sinking feeling that it was not going to be easy. It was an unpromising last day of the semester. I didn't expect a reply for 3 months. Since I had volunteered in Botany this summer, I expected a summer of light work and heavy lovemaking.

But, first I decided to take a run along the golf course. It was late, so I only went 5 miles. What I loved most about running, maybe more than the fields in the fading light, with the western meadowlarks pacing me from their nests in the gravel by the edge of the road to a safe distance, was the feeling of my muscles moving under the skin, flexing and loosening with each stride. Then it was time to run back. I showered at the gym and biked over to Gina's apartment.

The dinner Gina fixed, Soybean casserole, was great, seasoned with peppers and cayenne. I made the mistake of telling her that I had signed up in Botany for the fall.

What a night. I felt that I was arguing for my life, presenting a case that she should keep loving me. I strained, I reached, I listened, I answered, I tried to guess what she really meant. Finally she went into the bedroom and said she was going to write for an hour. So, I stayed in the kitchen, finished the dishes and started to paint. I forgot all about time. I was working on a study of a snake skeleton.

I felt her hands on my back, then my chest. I sighed and gave in to the reconnected electric current.

## 7 Sewing Machine: Letter to the Student Newspaper

Dear Spudnut Editor:

I went to a convention of the Academic Hearing Board a few days ago, as an observer. It reminded me of something Aldous Huxley said, that most people, most of the time, acted like a cross between a sewing machine and a toaster. How fortunate I was to observe both in action at once, in every member of the board! Where were the appliance repair people when we needed them?

~~E Moon~~ Ida ho ho'

## 8 Words without Knowledge? Report of the Hearing Board

May 22, 1975

Appeal of Walter Cant to the Academic Hearing Board
On May 15, 1975 the Academic Hearing Board convened a formal hearing to take oral testimony and receive written evidence on an appeal from Walter Cant, a graduate student in Philosophy. Attending the hearing were Cant, his advisor (Ellsin Moon), the members of Cant's thesis committee (Leigh Carson, Caesar Sam Finn, Ronn Kraft), and an observer from the Graduate School (Karen G. Hard). These proceedings were recorded on tape. This report, dated May 17, 1975, is a summary of the Board's findings and conclusion reached in an executive session immediately following the hearing. Attached to this report are two written statements from Cant (one submitted before and the other during the hearing) containing the charges directed at Cant's thesis committee.

The point upon which Cant placed greatest emphasis was that his major professor (Carson) gave oral and written approval to a finished thesis and Finn, according to Cant, had indicated previously that when Carson signed the thesis he (Finn) would also sign. Finn and Kraft then refused to sign the thesis and, Cant alleges, convinced Carson not to sign. Cant maintains that, in effect, the necessary majority of the thesis committee had accepted the thesis and the appellant should be awarded a master's degree. With regard to Carson's oral approval, Cant's account of the circumstances and wording of the alleged conversation is at best hazy. Carson denies that any such conversation or promise of approval occurred. To support the claim of a written commitment Cant relied entirely on a single sentence in a three page communication from Carson to Cant. This sentence reads, "I think I'm ready to sign this after I talk to Sam and Ronn." (See attached document labeled "7th Draft, Mar. 30. ) Carson notes that there are two qualifications in the sentence—"I think" and "after I talk to Sam and Ronn" —and that it is preceded by two pages of Carson's specific objections and followed by three general objections to the contents of the draft. Finn stated that his acceptance was always conditional on the thesis being presented in acceptable form. Neither Finn nor Kraft believed that this, or any earlier draft, was even minimally adequate. The Board does not perceive how any thing other than wishful thinking could have persuaded Cant that his thesis had been accepted.

Cant also charges that he was handicapped in writing and getting approval of his thesis by cursory, general, ambiguous and inconsistent guidance from the committee and Carson in particular. To buttress this complaint Cant selected some twenty odd pages of objections, suggestions, and comments made by

Carson at various stages and drafts of the thesis preparation. Carson noted, as did the Board, that these submissions are sufficiently extensive, specific,' clear, and consistent so that points and defects to which Carson took exception in early drafts are readily recognizable when the same points and defects recur in subsequent revisions, including the version presented by Cant as finished. At an early stage of the thesis Carson advised a change in format. Such a course is not unique to this instance. In fact, shifts in emphasis, format, scope, and even topic are more likely to be the rule than the exception in the preparation of theses and dissertations. The Board believes that this charge is without merit.

Cant also asserts that ultimately his work was not accepted solely because the members of the committee disliked the style of the thesis. Carson, Finn, and Kraft all agreed 'that while style was the determinant factor, they withheld approval on the basis of fundamental defects in the thesis and not on grounds of personal standards and preferences. The committee members pointed out, and supported, that although their suggestions on how to cope with these defects brought partial compliance, Cant in many instances ignored or defied repeated warnings that he must remedy the lack of lucidity, cogency, and coherency in his thesis. Whether or not the appellant considers lucidity, etc., to be matters of style, it is clear that he expected that the committee members were to accept Cant's judgments to when and to what degree it was necessary to make alterations in the manner of presentation. But Cant's actions went beyond intractability. By his own account, Cant willfully complicated the committee's task by attributing quotes in one draft by actual name and in subsequent drafts by a *nom de plume*. Cant also testified that he knew of errors—whether purposely or inadvertently made was not clear—in the thesis, which he had deliberately not removed in order to see if the mistakes would be detected. Cant recounted these episodes in terms and tones that made it obvious that to him they were pleasurable and meritorious. Not only did this make it difficult for the Board to give credence to Cant's statements offered in support of his allegations, but the ethics of such actions are at best questionable and indicate that Cant fails to comprehend the vast distinction between scholarship and gamesmanship.

By unanimous agreement the Board reached the following conclusions:

1. That Cant has not fulfilled his thesis requirement.
2. The thesis committee, and particularly Carson, constructively and conscientiously exercised their functions of advising and aiding Cant's work. Indeed, the members of the committee showed commendable forbearance. in view of Cant's uncooperative and obstructionist attitude and conduct.
3. From the beginning of the drafting process and consistently thereafter, the committee made known to Cant the minimum standards necessary for approval of the thesis. The decision to use his own standards and to ignore the admonitions of the committee was Cant's alone.

Responsibility for this decision and its consequences remains entirely with Cant.

4. Cant's thesis has not been definitively rejected. Rather he has been told by all three members of the committee that they have been and are still willing to sign a thesis in acceptable-form.

It was moved, seconded, and unanimously agreed by the members of the Academic Hearing Board that Cant's appeal is denied.

## 9 Making Love

I was surprised that the Board had decided so quickly. I wondered if they had read a single page. I answered their findings immediately, then went running. This time I took the old highway to Pullman, with its panoramic views of the fields.

As I started up the first hill to the old highway, I started to breathe hard. I slowed a bit. Then at the crest I sped up, and as I approached the first house I sprinted. Within seconds I heard barking and the dog came around the corner of the house. By then I had a large enough lead and speed to discourage him. When he turned around, I started slacking off, trying to find a rhythm and recapture my breath. Fortunately, that was the only unfenced dog on the route. Doubtless I would tempt him on the return trip also. I settled into rhythm of speeding up the hills and slowing on the downside. There were a lot of hills. It was the Palouse grassland, named by the French as being as comforting as the breasts of women—I have no idea what they were thinking when they named the Grand Titons, perhaps much younger women. I think I might want to live in France and study the phenomenology of French women.

I came back in the early afternoon and left a note for Gina in our secret place, "CG: Ace shelver requires torrid kiss from Sr. Secretary—Is today a supply day? I love you, WC"

Then, after I was finished working I went down and found her reply: "MW: Four kisses enough? Meet at the cola aisle after work. CG"

Gina and I met in the Safeway to pick out some broccoli. The cola aisle was where we met the first time (outside the library anyway). As a cola nut (sorry for the pun, I mean addict), I always started my shopping with the necessities, then got to the milk and vegetables. Gina has been trying to convert me to vegetarian, and I agree that it is healthier and more ethical, but most of the stuff we get as meat substitute seems like dirt seasoned with sand. On the other hand, the casseroles are great and highly seasoned.

The nice thing about that diet is that my body is nicely balanced for any activities after dinner, or after painting, or after a movie and a walk. Like tonight, which was a Friday. *The Rocky Horror Picture* was at one theater and *Jaws* at the other. I let her choose and she went with the least scary, although I was not sure which was which.

We walked back past the funeral home and the Moose bar, then under the full trees along Second Street.

I unbuttoned her skirt as we went up the stairs single-file. It fell off before the door and she had to get her keys out quickly. As I went in I threw my shirt over the couch. As I was leaning, she pushed me over the arm of the couch and said, "Stay!"

I heard the fridge door open and close. Her blouse was open as she came around the corner. I started to sit up but she straddled me and opened the lid of the ice cream. She scooped some with her from teeth and dropped it on my chest, then kissed me forcefully. As I pulled her to me, I could feel the cold melting between us. I could taste the ice cream on her teeth, but that melted immediately. I said it was melting down my chest. So, she looked at me licking her lips and plunged down to follow it. I had no idea what my brain was doing, but I remember everything my hands did, and everything her lips did. I pulled her up and delicately slid her panties to the side. She rose higher and pushed a breast towards my mouth. After a few hours—time had really slowed—I swung her back onto the couch and grabbed the box of ice cream. I dropped a mouthful on her belly button and followed it downhill. The joy of gravity!

After another few hours, we moved down the hall for a brief acrobatic combination, then into the bedroom. I still had my sox on; she still had her blouse over a shoulder. In bed we took these last things off, getting ice cream on the sheets as well. We made love more slowly, just moving slightly and kissing, holding and then pushing away and holding closer again. The subtlety of electricity!

Sometime in the night, we got up and gathered the sticky clothes and melted ice cream and put them in the tub with us. I pointed out that warm water is an aphrodisiac, although I didn't know that or care. I think that was the only time one of used breath on words. So we filled the tub and sat front to back until the water was cold and we had to refill it. The magic of fluids!

## 10 Passionate Words to the President

20 May 1975

President Garnet:
On April 7 of this year, I requested that an Academic Hearing Board (AHB) meet to hear an appeal in which I questioned whether my committee had followed normal procedures in prolonging my attempt to finish my Master of Arts thesis in Philosophy. On May 15, 24 hours after I secured legal aid and informed a number of people of this, the AHB suddenly agreed to meet (so suddenly that my advisor was unable to attend). After almost 4 hours of undirected incompetence and arrant prejudge on the part of the AHB, I was so upset that I immediately called Dr. Bono's office; later, after reaching him, I protested my treatment by the AHB, and inquired as to the next step in the appeal process. I was informed that even if it was found that the AHB was prejudiced, the case would either be reheard by that same AHB, or by the Faculty Council. Having tried for 12 months to work with my committee, having asked Dr. Strand to intercede, having sampled the curious operation of the AHB, and having realized the seemingly interminable political process ahead of me, as outlined by Dr. Bono, I have continued working with my committee: Professor Carson said that I should submit the entire thesis, and Dr. Finn has continued reading the introduction, and Mr. Kraft has not been located; in other words I am where I was last year at this time, and despair of finishing. The purpose of this letter is to correct the biased report of the AHB, and question the nebulous university policies on the responsibilities of graduate students and their faculty. Since the appeal is on tape, fortunately, I shall address my comments to that as well as to the AHB's formal written finding, and the amazing inconsistencies and errors in those findings.

The AHB alleges that it convened a formal hearing; this is a sad exaggeration: Professor Dodd, the chairman, opened it like a continuing bridge game, assuming that everyone present knew one another. Neither I nor Professor Moon were introduced. Only after Ellsin Moon's and my own obvious discomfort, did the AHB introduce itself. At first Professor Dodd and the other members were even unsure of the extent of their responsibilities and powers, although a refreshing glance at the appropriate pages of the handbook, as well as over a week to draft their reply (which I received May 26th) seemed to have helped their memory. Professor Dodd asked if the meeting could be informal; I agreed, on the condition that if disputes arose, then Robert's Rules of Order would be followed, as stipulated in the University Handbook; later, when disputes did occur, I was called down by him for insisting that these be followed, and held to be out of order—in a meeting notable for its *lack* of order and direction. No one on the AHB even tried to direct the course of the appeal; in the unequal encounter between a graduate student and his committee, the AHB immediately sided with its fellow faculty members, evading the issue, allowing irrelevant material and name-calling, and passing judgment with their own misdirected questions.

Specifically, the AHB begins its report with a typical misleading statement that my greatest emphasis was on Dr. Carson's oral and written approval of the 5th version of the 7th draft of my thesis, when indeed my emphasis was on the monumental aberration from department procedures by my committee, a small part of which was Dr. Carson's definite approval and subsequent change of mind after talking with "Sam and Ronn." The AHB completely ignored Dr. Finn's testimony on the normal procedures of his department; it blatantly ignored other of Dr. Carson's notes, including one in which he says that Dr. Finn told him that he would never read it, as it ignores the fact that Dr. Finn admitted to Dean Strand that he had only read 6 pages of the 7 drafts submitted to him in the previous year; it ignored Mr. Kraft's inability to remember anything at all about any of the drafts, choosing instead to minimize all of my evidence. For instance, their report finds that Dr. Carson's denial of approval was definite, whereas my ability to remember the circumstances and wording of the alleged conversation were hazy at best; the AHB's choice of sides cannot hide the fact that both my own and Dr. Carson's recollections were hazy, after all it was one of a number of such conversations, quiet and agreeable, and not a traumatic auto accident as Dr. Sooner treated it. The AHB also found it convenient to ignore the fact that both Finn and Kraft admitted intending to have signed if Carson signed, and that Carson did not challenge my offer to present two students whom he had told that he was going to sign my thesis (or perhaps only "thought" he would); furthermore, the AHB also ignored the fact that Dr. Carson did admit authorizing me to hire a typist, which I did, and that almost one-3rd of his comments are directions for the typist; is this the attitude of a professor who does not intend to sign? The AHB notes that I relied on a single sentence of acceptance from Dr. Carson; was more necessary? Dr. Carson's specific "objections", usually termed suggestions, were corrected within 2 hours of my receipt of the draft; his general objections resulted from consistent misunderstanding of my notation, and an inconsistent dislike for long (about 15 lines) quotes.

The AHB listened to some of Dr. Finn's testimony, that he felt it was inadequate, overlooking how little of it he had read. The AHB accepted Professor Kraft's allegations that I had deliberately fooled my committee at every turn and foiled their sincere attempts to help me. Mr. Kraft protested, contrary to all of his previous conversations with me, that he had read-all that he was offered, but strangely could not remember anything about any of the drafts, not one mistake, not one correction, not even the subject, and was reduced to parroting Dr. Carson's favorite term, "incoherent." How did Professors Finn and Kraft find reasons to judge the thesis inadequate when they never obviously read more than 9 pages between them?

I did find Dr. Carson's directions ambiguous and inconsistent, and so submitted **all** of her comments from the 4th through the 7th drafts, not selections of them as the AHB contends, having obviously failed to note their completeness. Dr. Carson, supported by the AHB, called her comments extensive—20 odd pages, 8 of which were 3x5 cards, over a period of 10 months, criticizing over 740 pages (surely not a very prodigious output on her part). She also admitted that she did not like reading it, citing her weak eyes.

Dr. Carson further claimed, as again did the AHB, that her clear, extensive submissions were not corrected in subsequent drafts, and to support her claim presented select portions, out of order, from the 4th draft, falsely presenting it as the 7th. In spite of my protests that examining nonsequential fragments of one draft was unfair, and irrelevant to the problem of procedure, the AHB, after cursorily, and in obvious confusion, glancing at these selections from one draft, was mysteriously able to observe that defects were uncorrected in other, unobserved drafts. The AHB refused to look at copies of the drafts 1 through 7, which I offered. Furthermore, what were these defects? No one was able to find grammatical or conceptual errors; did they refer to their dislike of the sentence arrangement? On the one section Dr. Finn read, on Aristotle, and judged to be incompetent, Dr. Carson commented in writing that she liked it, but when I mentioned that, she said that she really didn't read it well. Dr. Carson was unable to read correctly my letter to Dean Strand, alleging there were errors in it. There were no errors.

The AHB believes that changes in format, scope, emphasis, and topic are the rule, net the exception, but offered no instances, and ignored my testimony with Dean Strand and other Faculty members who felt otherwise. Perhaps one change is the case, or two, but I did 7 drafts using 3 modes of writing. Dr. Carson, in response to Professor Moon's question, admitted that he had encouraged me to write in the manner of Wittgenstein for two drafts, even though he felt that no graduate student in the U.S. or U.K. was capable of effectively succeeding at it. Was this just an exercise in impossibility, promoted by Dr. Carson for her own interests? Certainly these shifts are not typical of the Philosophy Department procedure, as described by Dr. Finn; as he succinctly outlined, using another graduate student (Eric Rhodes, who graduated in May, having begun his thesis at the same time) as an example: Eric finished one draft of his thesis, mailed it to Dr. Carson, who corrected the grammar and spelling, rewrote portions, and suggested changes. Dr. Finn and the 3rd member of the committee read it, and then Dr. Finn phoned Eric long distance to inform him of their suggestions, while all three signed the authorization to proceed with the final draft. As I have related earlier, this was not the case for my thesis; either it was not read, or directed through curious revisions.

On page 3 the AHB refers again to "fundamental defects," and claims that my committee pointed them out, and then supported their contentions. No such thing occurred on the tape, but the AHB submits that I ignored or defied them. This is the worst and most irresponsible fabrication of the AHB, which it enlarges by stating that I attempted to force the committee to accept my judgments on alterations, that I went beyond intractability in complicating the task with nom de plumes and deliberate errors. I did, with complete truthfulness, admit that when Dr. Carson objected to my poetry, I attributed the same poems to my own registered allonyms, which she then found not only acceptable but apropos. I also testified that in the 7th draft I found a large—covering 11 pages—error that had been carried through 4 drafts, and which not even I had noticed, so in my distress I left it unmentioned to see if it would be detected. Since Professor Finn and Carson teach ancient philosophy, if they did not notice it, either they read it haphazardly, or were unable to detect it. Perhaps it was juvenile of me to test my professors in this way, but at least I am mature enough to admit my mistakes. Because not one of my committee admitted to making any indiscretions, mistakes, slanders, or possibly mishandling my thesis, the AHB seems to have used my errors in judgment as an excuse for overlooking any inexcusable and inexplicable behavior on the part of my committee.

The AHB condemned my attitude as unethical, mistaking my cynicism and despair for pleasure and meritoriousness; does the AHB honestly believe that working 20 hours a day for 250 days to produce over 1100 pages in 7 complete drafts was for the purpose of fooling my professors? Does the AHB think that I enjoyed such strenuous frustration so much that I required medical attention? The AHB does not give credence to my statements, with their admission of my possible faults as a student, but it is able to accept the entirely one-sided presentation of my committee, each of whom claimed to have acted perfectly, even in the face of written and verbal evidence to the contrary. The completely bigoted conclusions of the AHB indicate that it fails to comprehend the vast distance between scholarship and politics.

> And what are these conclusions, reached by unanimous agreement? They are:
> (1) Somehow, having not read more than unconnected fragments of one draft, or even admittedly been able to understand even the conversation about it, the AHB was able to conclude that I had not fulfilled my thesis requirement, thus fulfilling a function which it claimed it did not have.
> (2) Somehow the AHB, after ignoring pertinent testimony, concluded that my committee, in spite of being handicapped by frequent changes of direction, or not having read it, "constructively and conscientiously exercised their functions of advising and aiding" my work, though apparently without a trace. Indeed it said that the committee

showed "commendable forbearance in view of my uncooperative and obstructionist attitude and conduct," an attitude that caused me to implore them to read any of it, that literally begged for advice and direction and conduct represented by 1100 pages in 7 drafts and numerous revisions, some typed at further expense, and all Xeroxed and offered to each of the committee.

(3) Somehow the AHB concluded that I ignored the minimum standards transmitted, however nebulously, by the committee, and substituted my own, but how can this be? My own standard, as exercised in only one draft, is mystical verse. Dr. Carson's standards were prose, Wittgensteinian Lebensforms, and more prose, and her directions were followed in 6 of 7 drafts (Professors Finn and Kraft actually offered none). I begged for standards that were never offered. The AHB is certainly inventive. I strictly followed the programs outlined by my major professor, and made all of the changes that he actually advised.

(4) My complaint was never that the thesis was definitely rejected, but that although the committee has been willing to sign it in acceptable form, it has no consistent idea of what is acceptable form, and has not read it closely enough, if at all, to determine if it is in acceptable form.

In summary, the AHB used improper, informal procedures to allow itself to be prejudiced by irrelevant information; it chose what evidence suited its predetermined decision, and used my mistakes to excuse those of my committee; in playing faculty politics, it assumed grotesque posturings to preserve the monumental egos bruised by a simple questioning of their whimsical methods, disdaining its function as a hearing board, and demonstrating behavior unsuited to members of a faculty council. The AHB demonstrated a curious lack of integrity, in allowing my own committee, when it could not answer my contentions, to call me a liar, charlatan, and incompetent, to falsely accuse me of plagiarism, trickery, and obstruction. Mr. Kraft was especially slanderous in this respect, misrepresenting facts, accusing me of running behind the scenes to fool everyone. Instead of acting on a concise, well-ordered, and well-documented complaint, the AHB chose to accept misrepresented and irrelevant information, which it was not competent to judge in any case, and which it misinterpreted, to judge the thesis, in Dr. Carson's words, "incoherent," 'too radical," and "too poetic."

As I have stated earlier, I am now trying for the eighth time to complete a draft that is satisfactory to my committee; I am no further along than I was last June, though my committee regards me now as dangerously ungrateful, in addition to its previous views of me as temperamental and intractable. Having sampled the political process at this university, I am unable to face its jaundiced trials, and will not make another appeal, both to avoid further frustration and to prevent members of the faculty from compromising themselves again; instead this is a letter of disclosure, to be read in conjunction with my original request, the AHB, and the taped hearing. I am sad that these circumstances could have occurred at all, and I hope that this letter may contribute towards preventing such unbalanced situations in the future.

Sincerely,
Walter Cant

Cant after the Hearing

## 11 Trees in Vats

June 1

I walked across to the biology building, which was across the street from the Admin building, the home of Philosophy. This building is a large rambling many-times-added-to green stone building. I took the stairs to the second floor to Loren's office. He was taking notes in a bound notebook, so I seated myself on one of the two wooden captains chairs under his bookcase. I scanned the titles and picked out a book on silviculture by Tourney and started looking at the contents.

Loren said, without looking up, "That's too old. We use Hawley now."

I picked up the Hawley and looked at the table of contents; it was all cutting and management—no science, no trees, no ecology. I wondered.

"Let's go into the lab and orientate you."

I was familiar with the lab, having worked with Chuck on his lichen project during the spring, but I went along and was reacquainted with the instruments.

I kept thinking of the irony of working to process trees into paper with industrial methods to provide material for theses and dissertations. We should go back to talking and just producing a few scrolls by the masters, not the students.

Back in the office, he seemed pleased with my familiarity with the equipment and was expanding on his project.

"The CutQuick Timber Corporation is paying for this. They realize that soon we will have cut all the old-growth timber, even the good stuff in the National Parks. But, we don't care about that old stuff anymore, we can go hi-tech on it. And, that is what this project is—the answer to America's timber shortfall. We can grow wood in vats, perfect wood, without knots or flaws, any length, with any grain."

"But, how can you stress it for strength without gravity or competition?" I asked.

Loren answered immediately, "Excellent question." Then he paused for a while to fiddle with his glasses. "Of course, we can grow the fibers to any length in the vats. However, getting them to interconnect … hmmm. Well, we will be able to introduce glues at the proper time. I want you to go over to Milken's lab and see what they are doing with pressed wood. The glues are fantastic. That stuff is stronger than plywood and nicer than beams. Meanwhile, look over my design for the vat and see if you can see if anything is missing."

And, so began my introduction to PerfectWood.

## 12 The Committee of Three Meets Godzilla and Mothra

June 19, in the President's Office.

"Thank you, President Garnet. I know Vice President Bono, Dean Strand, and of course, Professors Finn, Carson, and Kraft," I said, wondering why I was invited without Walter. We were meeting in the President's office on the ground floor of the Administration Building. The room looked like a men's club, or maybe I was thinking of the Men's Club Bar and Grill at the Crescent Department store in Spokane, with paneled dark wood walls and a worn oriental carpet. I'd heard that the administrative offices were to be remodeled. We sat at a large round oak table. Hunter Garnet was a small woman with beautiful eyes and curly hair and a reserved dignified demeanor. V. P. Bono was a large, bluff, aggressive, slightly addled, male with a mane of white hair, his only concession or claim to dignity. Dean Strand was a tall vital person. I had never met Strand and Bono before. The committee of three was slouched in their chairs like kids in the principal's office.

Garnet: I've got a letter of appeal from a Walter Cant, a graduate student, concerning a hearing board meeting, and various items he's expressing concern about. Now, one of you, please tell me what is going on here? Caesar?

Finn: I'm afraid I committed the original sin in the Cant affair, as I said in my letter to you Hunter, when I supported his candidacy for admittance to Graduate School, in spite of all his deficiencies. I should have made my support contingent upon his getting help from the Counseling Center. Obviously possessing ability, he just as obviously needs some kind of psychological help if he could seriously claim 122 college credits when in fact he had only 64, umm, plus 3. He also had 23 chapel deficiencies from the University of the South. My original error, then, invited more of the same. Although Dean Strand had not acted on Mr. Cant's application to Graduate School (since the admission procedure had not been completed), Walter assumed that he had, and continued work on his M.A. in Philosophy.

Strand: Ahem, actually, Caesar, I did admit him. The letters from Carson and Dodge were excellent, and yours was, err, umm, not completely against it.

Finn: You did? I thought it was later. Oh. Anyway, he completed the Spring Semester 74 and Summer Session 74 under the assumption that he was, or was just about to be, a graduate student, and began work on his thesis that summer.

In the meantime Mr. Yount had established by phone call that Mr. Cant had **not** been admitted to the University of Massachusetts as claimed on his Application for Admission Form, and Mr. Yount proposed canceling his registration. We—I—had been well-compromised by this time—Walter's rationalizations have a certain charm—and recommended admitting him, treating the matter as a mistake rather than a falsification. I repeated this recommendation when Dean Hard made inquiries.

Carson: Have you heard anything since?

Garnet: Ellsin, you're his counsel. Do you know anything about his background?

Moon: Not counsel actually. Well, not at first. But I confess a certain interest now. I don't know anything about his background—well, much. I haven't seen transcripts. But, he seems well-versed in the fields he says he has had courses in. He showed me an article, of which he was fifth author. It was on astronomy, the stellar structure of carbon stars I think, so I would have no reason to doubt that he took courses in it.

Finn: Who published it?

Moon: *Astrophysical Letters*, I think.

Finn: Humfh. As for the horrendous tale of drafts is concerned, it is an extension of the same problem; inability to see the world as others see it, or words to that effect. At least one of the 'drafts' is a paste-job, courtesy of the Xerox machine and previous drafts. Another draft is entirely in poetic form; certainly an original approach to solving the problem of clarity, but one which he had been told would be unacceptable. My original work with him had been an attempt to get him to clearly formulate the issue or problem on which he intended to write before going with the complete work; after two or three unsatisfactory attempts to get it clearly stated, he decided to work with Professor Carson on his thesis.

Carson: All right. I decided to give him his head, and let him do the complete thesis before commenting. Walter then did a great deal of writing, but still failed to follow correction or criticism. He refused to make grammatical corrections or seek coherence between the various parts. He felt these, our, directives were unduly restrictive.

Finn: Yes, rather than correct or re-write, he would try a whole new approach. In as much as the thesis topic concerns poetic insight to being, criticism of the thesis often was dismissed on the handy grounds that the critic 'lacked' poetic insight. In other words, it was not a question of our refusing to give help, but of Walter's refusing to accept help.

Moon: Professor Finn, I'm not sure it will turn out to be so simple—at least to anyone examining all the evidence.

Garnet: What do you mean, Ellsin?

Moon: I'm not sure that anyone has looked at all the evidence.

Finn: I believe his committee has.

Moon: Have you gotten to page four yet, Caesar?

Finn: I believe you're just an observer here.

Garnet: Ladies and Gentlemen. We must conclude this matter agreeably.

Carson: Since the denial of his appeal to the Academic Appeals Board, Cant

## The Thesis

seems to have gotten the message and is finally getting the thesis into shape.

Finn: Past experience would suggest that we are being unduly optimistic, but perhaps the odds are in our favor this time. At any rate, I would appreciate it Hunter if you would accept nothing that he writes to you at its face value, but if you deem it important enough, make a private examination, or have him take it to a hearing board.

Kraft: The Academic Board spent three and one half hours listening to everything Walter had to say, and found every claim invalid. He was allowed to say anything he wanted to say, which he did, except that he was not allowed to interrupt others who were responding to his charges, which he did anyway.

Garnet: Then what was wrong with the hearing? Why is he appealing to me?

Finn: Nothing was wrong with the hearing. He objects that the board found in our favor and not his.

Moon: The hearing had obvious shortcomings. Nothing like that ever would have held up in a court of law or—

Finn: It wasn't a court of law.

Moon: Or a formal academic review.

Strand: I encouraged him to ask for the hearing, based on what he told me about his problems with his thesis.

Finn: Why didn't you come to me?

Strand: I did. You did say you only read three pages of everything he's written.

Finn: Oh, yes. That meeting. I didn't realize that he'd bamboozled you into believing him.

Bono: He lost the appeal. Let's do nothing. Let him start over.

Moon: (Cordoner R. Bono, a weak and silly name, infertile letters despite their shape: 'o corn red robot,' 'born to corrode.')

Strand: Since I recommended the appeal, let me try to convince him to return to the committee and do what you want.

Carson: I don't think I want him back. He made his own mess, nest, let him lie in it.

Kraft: I think we could get him through if we managed to control him. I'm willing to outline the steps for him to follow to complete the degree.

Strand: Remember, Sam. If you guys want to stay accredited, you have to have more people graduate with the Philosophy major or with a masters.

Finn: We have two more promising graduate students coming up. That should not be a problem.

Strand: Why did you ever admit Cant, then?

Finn: It was a problem two years ago. We needed another face.

Bono: Then why pamper one bad egg? Let him go on to something else. We don't need to go out of our way on this.

Moon: Perhaps if you could ask him to abridge the last draft. (Cono, Bono,

Rono. It's the old 'odor bob con,' oldest smell in the—)

Garnet: Does this wrap it up, then? Ellsin? You have anything to add? No? Okay, am I going to get any more letters crying foul on this thing?

Finn: I think not.

Carson: I hope not.

Kraft: I'll outline the rules and get copies out to everyone.

Garnet: Very well. Let's get on with it, shall we?

Gymnastics Grass Area

## 13 Going swimming

The summer promised to be another perfect season. I ran every day, I swam every day, and Gina and I seemed to have settled into a domestic routine of writing, painting, and lovemaking, punctuated from time to time with new recipes to cook. Five days a week, I spent hours grinding up different kinds of wood and preparing a 'soup' of the fibers. We had built 4 minivat models about a meter long each and plumbed them into separate water systems. One days a week I devoted to editing the thesis. However, I was so pleased with most of it, that I started sending it out to a few academics with interest in phenomenology, as well as to a few publishers who had issued books in the subject area, Routledge & Kegan Paul.

We have settled into a habit already—of sleeping together all weekend (except for Saturday morning when I have to hide my stuff in the closet in case her mother comes by to go shopping). Sometimes we make love on week nights, but she chases me away so she can study; just as well, since I ought to study also.

The gymnastics club was a lot of fun. We worked out at lunchtime a few days a week. When we couldn't get the equipment set up (it was in the women's gym and they were very proprietary of the space), we would practice on the lawn between the Admin and the gym. The lawn rolled gracefully down from the Admin hill to the gym, so it was possible to get some good acceleration for tumbling and somersaults.

I always went running late in the afternoon, with Rex from the Library. If it was late, sometimes Gina would accompany us on her bicycle. She sometimes had trouble on the gravel of the old highway, but near campus, where it changed to asphalt, she could sail down the hills. Then on Saturday, we would ride from Simplotville to Huntington (named after the railroad magnate who passed through and impressed the locals so much they named the town after him), get a milkshake at the Cow College and then raid their orchard for McIntosh apples. Then slowly ride back uphill to our town (named after the potato giant who never passed through, thus impressing the locals—these locals, remember, were mostly people who thought the area was waste grassland, unsuitable for farming or grazing, and many of them thought they were settling in Oregon or Utah).

I usually went swimming at noon or in the evening, but this summer I decided to take a class in advanced swimming to learn any new techniques with some of the strokes. Sure enough, someone had figured out that the butterfly was faster if you put an extra movement of both hands on the pushing stroke. It seemed to work. The class forced me to have a little more discipline. And, it was far more competitive than recreational swimming or just lap swimming.

Despite my misgivings, I was learning a lot about the biochemistry of wood, and my arm strength was increasing from the interminable grinding. Somehow, however, we just could not get the wood to grow. Loren was balancing various growth hormones, and I was finessing the broth with minerals and nutrients. I sometimes wondered whether this was a good idea. If he succeeded, then would trees and forests become more valuable or less valuable? Would it put more pressure on wild forests or less?

There were some costs that we were not including in our calculations, for instance the relatively high amount of pollution from rinsing the vats. With any kind of jump in scale that would be a monstrous environmental problem. In fact, shrimp fisheries in southeast Asia were beginning to see how bad pollution could be from shrimp farms.

The Administration Lawn

## 14 Desperate Words to the President

16 July 1975

Dear President Garnet:
This morning I was allowed to inspect my graduate records for the first time. I read, for the first time, a note written to you by Professor Caesar Finn, dated 24 June 1973. I am astounded as much by its condescending tone as by its flagrant misdirection. Therefore, although I expect no action to be undertaken by you, I am writing to answer his note, point by point, to correct my record at the Graduate School.

In the first sentence, Dr. Finn takes responsibility for the "Cant affair" as if it were some tawdry scandal on my part, since, he says, he supported my candidacy for graduate school. In January 1974, at the advice of Dr. Carson, and against the express wishes of Dr. Finn, I applied to the graduate school. Dr. Finn did write a letter to the graduate school, in which he cast aspersions on my character and labeled me temperamental—a judgment he formed instantly, upon hearing that I had dropped out of school a number of times, without bothering to inquire further into the circumstances. Although he admitted my ability in that letter, nowhere in it does he recommend, or even support, my admission. No wonder he was surprised that I received a notice of acceptance later that week in January. In this same first sentence in his note to you, he mentions deficiencies; yet the only deficiency I was asked to make up in required course work was one class in Ancient Philosophy. True, I have no degree, but I have easily demonstrated my learning by other, more objective criteria; for instance, my graduate record aptitude scores total 1490, a sum that places me in the top one percent of all college graduates.

In the second sentence, Dr. Finn implies that I needed help from the counseling service; if not libel, the statement is in poor taste.

In the third sentence, he judges that I need help if I could claim 122 credits, instead of the 67 he assigned me. Actually a close examination of all the course work I have taken reveals over 200 credits; unfortunately, for whatever reasons, over half of these were 'F's, although many of these were later removed, or changed to withdrawals or audits, by administrators sympathetic to my financial or family problems (regardless, I learned enough to get credit later for many courses by written examination). I believe Dr. Finn's figure is erroneous.

In the fourth sentence, Dr. Finn admits to further errors; I must concur.

In the fifth sentence, he says that Dean Strand had not acted on my admission. If not, why do I have an informal note of acceptance from him dated 28 January 1974, as well as the formal notice with a later date? If not, why was

I allowed to form a Master's Committee in February, with Dr. Carson as my major professor? Perhaps Dr. Finn forgot. In any case, I assumed nothing, and proceeded on the standard course only after express written instructions.

In the sixth sentence in the first paragraph, Dr. Finn mentions that I completed the spring and summer under that same "assumption." I didn't just complete the semesters. I aced them (3.94 gpa). In May 1974, I wrote a 40-page paper for Dr. Carson, on "Merleau-Ponty's Aesthetics," on which she wrote "Best paper thus far....this ought to be the basis of an M.A. thesis—I would like a copy." Dr. Carson and I began our study of Merleau-Ponty at the same time, the fall of 1974. She was working on a project and was too busy, and as Dr. Finn offered to help me, I rewrote and expanded that paper and submitted it to him. He rejected that first six pages and refused afterwards to read the remaining ones. Even though I confined myself afterwards to other courses, I was given a 'passing/in progress' grade for my thesis course. Why, if as he now contends, I was not performing satisfactorily?

In the first sentence of the 2nd paragraph, Dr. Finn claims that "Mr. Yount had established by phone call that Mr. Cant had **not** been admitted to the University of Massachusetts as claimed on his Application for Admission Form, and Mr. Yount proposed canceling Mr. Cant's registration." That is false! What Mr. Yount established was that my file at the University of Massachusetts could not be located, in spite of their efforts to find it, and in spite my letters to them listing the courses I could remember, some of the professors, and even some of the students. Although I offered my complete correspondences to both Mr. Yount and Dr. Finn, both said that it wasn't necessary. At various times, I have pointed out other errors in my file here: for instance my high school record at Boston, Massachusetts is not only incomplete, but incorrect in places (it lists me as having 3 years of Spanish, when I had 4 of Latin). Also, two psychology courses taken in the fall of 1969 are missing from the transcript from NYU; then again, there are universities where I took courses that aren't even represented in the file. I have been told by Yount, and Finn, and Strand that it doesn't matter, since all that course work was in astrophysics or psychology.

In the 2nd sentence, Dr. Finn writes that he has been compromised, but I fall to see how, unless it is by his own questionable actions. Certainly I have not even attempted to rationalize anything. Why would I falsify a record containing Fs, as at NYU, or a record admittedly irrelevant to my career as a philosopher, as at Massachusetts? Dr. Finn interprets facts strangely. I have made neither mistakes or falsifications, and I regard Mr. Finn's accusations as libel.

I have no comment on the 3rd sentence, in which Dr. Finn repeats his recommendation to Dean Hard.

Beginning with the first sentence of the 3rd paragraph, he sees the horrendous tale of the drafts as an extension of my "inability to see the world as others see it." While I hope that I see the world differently from others, it usually isn't called an inability. In the next two sentences, Dr. Finn takes on the problem of the drafts, citing a "paste job," and one in verse. What Dr. Finn failed to mention was that they were all paste jobs to some extent. Since I do not know how to type, I hired a typist for most of the drafts. After a draft was finished, and two copies of it xeroxed for Finn and Kraft, the portions approved by Dr. Carson were used to form the core of the next draft. Dr. Carson approved the method. The draft in poetic form was done, as I have admitted repeatedly, for my own satisfaction. After it went completely unread even by Carson, as I expected, I began a 3rd draft on my own accord, based on the first given to Dr. Finn, which he had not only not criticized, but had not used to help me formulate the issue, as he has falsely written. After I submitted the 3rd draft in November of 1974, Dr. Carson returned it with the contents written on it that it was excellent, with short, pithy statements and perhaps I should try Wittgenstein's format. At no time did Dr. Carson give me my head —she refused even to look at the poetic draft — and at no time did I write without specific *written* directions from Dr. Carson. I made **all** corrections and accepted **all** criticisms, unless I was able to support my position in a manner satisfactory to Dr. Carson. Finn and Kraft did not read any of these drafts.

Mr. Finn states that I refused to make grammatical corrections, or to seek coherence, that I felt those directives to be restrictive. This is not true; the few grammatical correctives needed were made immediately. The members of the committee erroneously identified complex sentences as run-on sentences. Professor Carson religiously changed all semicolons to periods. Ability in English is sadly lacking in all the members of the Committee. Unable to find real mistakes, they have attempted to force their own style on the thesis. Several graduates in English have read through it and found that the most repeated mistakes were split infinitives, a minor breach uncaught by Carson and the Committee. Contrary to Dr. Finn I corrected and rewrote to avoid further new approaches suggested by Professor Carson.

Although the thesis does concern poetic insight, I never dismissed criticisms due to the lack of insight of the critic, but now that Dr. Finn mentions it, perhaps that explains some of the thesis's incoherence for him. What I did question, and question even more now, is the preparation of my professors: Mr. Kraft admitted a lack of interest as well as a lack of knowledge; Dr. Finn admitted (to myself, Dean Strand, and the Academic Hearing Board) reading only six pages each, from the seven drafts offered him, and that he knew nothing about, and intended not to learn anything about, phenomenology, although to his credit, he did read a short article on Merleau-Ponty, which allowed the thesis to appear more coherent to him, strangely enough. Dr. Carson apparently stopped reading Merleau-Ponty's works in the fall of 1975, and lost interest in the thesis, which has resulted in her many mistaken "corrections," and her inability even to recognize the later philosophies of Merleau-Ponty or Heidegger. In other words, to reverse Dr. Finn's last sentence of the 3rd paragraph, it wasn't a question of my refusing help, it was a question of their offering erroneous and contradictory help.

Since the denial of my petition by the Academic Hearing Board, my Committee began actively discharging its responsibilities; they met for the first time, and everyone actually read much—but not all—of the thesis. Dr. Carson read the most of it, and after changing her mind twice, decided to accept select chapters of it. However, they required another rough draft before the final rough draft, in violation of their previous agreement. I am not optimistic that these professors will suddenly acquire consistency and integrity, but I am hopeful that they can be gently forced to keep their word.

After the Academic Hearing Board refused to follow *Robert's Rules of Order*, in direct violation of the *Faculty Handbook of Policy and Procedure*, and after they refused to limit discussion to the pertinent issues, the meeting degenerated into a one-sided attack, faculty versus student, with Dean Hard falling asleep. Much to my disgrace, I defended myself against every irrelevant or false charge and character assassination. Obviously, since I was the only honest person there, and the only one to admit any mistakes, the Board became confused and found me totally at fault, ignoring significant evidence to the contrary. The university has met its flawless reputation for mutual teat sucking among its faculty.

In principle, I agree with the first sentence in the last paragraph, that you accept nothing that I write at face value. For that reason, I can offer written evidence (in Finn's, Carson's and Kraft's handwriting), witnesses, and tape-recorded support for **every** statement in this letter of correction. Furthermore, I expect you to extend the same consideration to Dr. Finn. And what proof does he have for his half-truths, no-truths, misrepresentations, and libel—beyond an insistent and prejudiced opinion?

Throughout this situation I have asked Dean Strand for advice—beginning with Mr. Finn's unethical down-grading of my papers, through the AHB miscarriage, and then about impartial referees for my thesis—and I have almost always followed it. I think he described the situation in these terms once: graduate students should be treated as peers, since their research in the field of their thesis is often in advance of their professor's, but they are often not. Dr. Finn and the rest of my Committee have violated that expectation by treating me like an imbecilic child. I am not. I am highly disciplined in every sense, physically, emotionally, and intellectually. I have worked full-time to put myself through school, and have become accomplished in a number of areas, academic and nonacademic. I intend to be treated fairly from now on, by the very rules of the University, and with its avowed high purpose. If you do not deem this matter important enough for consideration, and I find that no progress is being made before November 1st, I will use every academic and legal option available to me to conclude this 'affair.'

Sincerely
Walter B. Cant

## 15 Moving Together

Note #438: To Gina, Aspasia to my Pericles, Leontium to my Epicurus, Hypatia to my Orestes, Helen to my Goethe. This offering is your true present—not pen on paper, but my soul inscribed on your being, my shadow on your heels. Love, WC.

> Wisdom is a wild thing like the Arcadian doe
> And not easily captured with words. The dappled
> Form leaves its shadow in our grasp while it slips
> Away …

I had only been in my apartment on Harrison for three months, but it was perfect. It came furnished with oak and maple furniture, so that all I had to add was books, a few book cases, stereo, and my large easel for painting. I set up the easel in the kitchen, which had a classic (meaning really old and temperamental) refrigerator and a stove on four legs like the hut of Baba Yaga. I painted the walls a light yellow; the drapes were dark red. I could sit at my large desk and survey my readings while listening to music.

It was on the second floor with its own entrance. The other half of the upstairs was another one bedroom apartment with a separate entrance. A Professor of Psychology lived there with her cat, who was being trained to use the toilet, so the Prof could save on kitty litter perhaps. The cat seemed happy when she was outside.

So, I was pleasantly surprised and unpleasantly conflicted when Gina suggested that we move into her apartment on Second Street to save on rent. I had been staying there on weekends for a year, so I knew that I liked it. It had a working fireplace, although the bedroom and kitchen were smaller. It also had the advantage of being a block from downtown, rather than twelve blocks, like mine. It had a back yard, also, and rooms in the basement for storage. We discussed all of this after I presented my counteroffer that she move in with me.

When I agreed, she presented me with an airline ticket to Florida. Her parents had invited us to go in mid-November at the Thanksgiving break, so we would not miss any classes. And, then we celebrated in our typical way, on the magic couch, then across the magic floor towards the magic fireplace—and then the magic dimension that can be reached only with an athletic, intellectual and ethical love.

The moving was nothing but work. Her landlord had a truck, so we moved everything. I put my desk and some bookcases in unoccupied studio in the basement. I started fixing it up, and agreed to pay $20 a month for storage. It had a bathroom, but no kitchen. It had water damage and a lot of trash. It was going to be a longer project than anticipated.

I set up the easel in her kitchen, on the condition that she could use it. My clothes fit in the small hall closet. What we did not know was that we would soon be married by Idaho common law.

Walter's Old Apartment

## 16 Numbers

I was shelving in the 'BH's when Ellsin came by. I rarely saw her out of her office or beyond the first floor, so I was curious. I surreptitiously put down the book on aesthetics and greeted her with my latest bitch and rant about school.

"I'm still upset at getting a 'P' for the thesis course."

"Well, at least it is not a number," she said.

"Why? What do you mean?"

"The numbers we attach to grades are false quantities, unreal things."

"Right, the quantification of the unquantifiable."

"We quantify the quality of thought with a number, so that we can assess learning behavior; but, then it becomes a judgment of worth. We have William Farish to thank to that."

"Who?" I asked, always amazed at the facts that a Librarian can assemble in forty short years of reading.

"A tutor named William Farish suggested grading students' papers at Cambridge University in 1792. And that opened the floodgate of numbers. Later, others tried to quantify love, hate, and beauty, as Francis Galton did in Britain, Galton also proposed to quantify boredom, sanity and prayers. Then he counted the number of fidgets in church to see if women and children, oh never mind."

"I think the US Military Academy used numbers for grades after that."

"Yes, exactly. This pretends to makes an objective assessment of performance. But, at the same time, it introduces competition, and that reflects the old ideas of evolution, where competition was thought the basic interaction.

"Which of course contributes to a strictly physical, mathematical concept of reality, but—"

"Right, each tool has an ideological bias, as skills or behaviors are amplified or ignored. To a man with a hammer, everything looks like a nail. To a woman with a grade sheet, every one looks like a number, to a man with a computer everything is data, to a woman with a camera everything is an image.

"What if we changed the rules? Had the students grade faculty."

"After we reduce everything to grades and numbers, only those are real."

"Corrupt, insane, but real."

"Better yet, just eliminate grades."

"And part of the larger civilized ways, like writing and storing."

"Everything was also organized around writing; it is the grammocentric principle. This is also the foundation of modern management (as well as the source of the problem of plagiarism)."

"Don't get me started on copying and imitation."

## 17 Epistemology of Plants

Just like starting over. I was prepared for the fall, but somewhat cautious guardedly, since I had to change half of my spring courses to 'L's to avoid anything below a 'B.'

Registration was faster than ever. They had it in the giant Kibblesford dome. A trip to the bookstore forced me to get another student loan just to afford the botany books; one had 900 pages without a single photograph, just drawings.

The first classes went well. One of the professors, Eric, apparently was an artist and drew beautiful renditions in colored chalk of any plants he was teaching about. I had worked on Dr. Amundsen's lichen project so I was happy to have a class from him. Except for one casual goof-off prof, who was rebuilding his motorcycle in his living room and was always asking for help, the professors in this discipline seemed more competent and professional. I could not decide if that was because the subject was harder or easier.

I have been reading about the epistemology of plants, and I don't know what other word to use. Pine trees, for instance, pump a thick resin to supply growing central needles in the spring, when pests are rare. As it gets warmer, sawflies, small hovering insects, start to hatch their larvae on the pine, using the nutrient-rich resin in the central needles. When the tree registers the loss of resin in the inner needles, it starts to pump the resin to the outer needles, where wasps and birds can easily see and dine on the sawflies.

Trees have the chemical ability to register the quadrant where insects are taking too much sugar or resin. The willow tree, for instance, when under attack by some bugs, can pump stores of a precursor chemical to the bark in that region. Aspirin beetles follow the chemical. When other insects interact with the Aspirin beetles, they then spray aspirin gas to defend themselves, defending the willow in the process.

Plant root nodules can be caused by a cluster of bacteria feeding on sugars created by leaves and sent to nourish the roots. If the bacteria do give back or exchange useful chemicals, then that stimulates the plant to lure more of them with more sugar, otherwise, the plant can withdraw the sugar entirely from that root. When under attack by unfriendly fungi that does not give anything useful to the plant, the plant can spray ethylene gas from their roots. This spreads through soil, irritating the fungi and letting other plants start to prepare their own defenses.

## 18 Found Art: Letter to the Student Newspaper

September 27

Dear Spudnut Editor:

Espied I it on my way to class. It hunkered into the pavement by the student union, as if embarrassed by its own lack of symmetry or meaning, a misshapen blob of metal and dirt, unrelated to its surroundings, disconnected from any theoretical or ~~autistic~~ artistic foundation. There are those that criticize this kind of art, saying that the artist exercised no vision and little discipline, other than signing it and pocketing the fee.

Not only will I defend such art, but I urge the expansion of the category to include my own contribution to art, "found art." For example, later that same day, I saw a perfect example of an organic torroidal concretion left on the sidewalk, unique in its textural composition and forceful in its ontological presence. Delicate in its compositional harmony. Discrete in its colors—so many shades of brown and grey. Multidimensional. It was a veritable metaphor of the complexity and brevity of life, a celebration of the joy of eating and excreting. It was shit.

True, shit. But art is coprophilous as well as abstractly symbolic. And this expression was as evocative as the pile of metal and dirt seen in the morning. Can we not recognize the art in everything, and respect it?

~~W. B. Cant~~ The Wizard of ID

## 19 Two Mortals Visit God and an Archangle

October 20, 1975

We were back in the President's office meeting with the Dean and the President. The carpet had just been torn up, showing the wide pine floors underneath, clean but worn. The pine had probably come from Idaho's forests in the days when white pine was going for match sticks and buildings. It was a quiet morning. Garnet was a polite host and welcomed us to his office.

Garnet: I'm sure we all know each other: Dean Strand, Ellsin, Walter. I agreed to this meeting against my better judgment. I see the first item on my agenda is Cant putting his thesis in the library collection. Would you care to explain that, Mr. Cant?

Cant: No, it's not—

Strand: I am offended that you would try something so low after all the effort we have invested in trying to get you through school. I have phoned the Associate Director of the library and ordered him to remove the work. Furthermore, I am—

Cant: Excuse me, Dean Strand, but I did not submit a *thesis* to the library, I merely—

Strand: Then what was it?

Cant: I was—I only presented the library with a copy of a book *manuscript* for special collections, which they bound and catalogued. The head of special collections thought it would be a good addition. Furthermore, it was not offered as a thesis—in fact, the word 'thesis' does not appear on it. Neither was it offered as an official publication of the library. In listing—

Strand: Then why is—does the—do the words University Library appear under your name?

Cant: I placed my department underneath my name. This is a standard practice at most universities. I phoned the graduate school, publications office, and the university attorney first, before adding it. I am sure that my use of this format as well as the gift of my manuscript to the library is not in violation of any extant university regulations.

Strand: Whom did you talk to in the graduate school?

Cant: The secretary.

Strand: Well—

Cant: It's standard for authors to list their affiliations on the title page.

Garnet: I think, as long as its a gift to the library, the library should decide where to—what to do with it.

Moon: We have put it on the shelf, catalogued with phenomenology books.

## The Thesis

Strand: I don't want that thing to be in the open stacks. It's going to cause trouble and maybe set a bad precedent. I (sigh), that wasn't what I was told by Leigh.

Moon: (I wonder if Walter shouldn't be taking a course in crisis management.)

Garnet: Let's get on, then. Walter, what did you mean about legal options in your letter? Surely none will be necessary.

Cant: I hope not.

Garnet: Why don't you present your case to me?

Cant: On 6 January 1975, I'm sure you remember, I finished an expansion of the third draft of a thesis, as directed by my advisor. All of us were so certain that all of the department's requirements had been met that Professors Carson and Finn approved my taking a full—20 hours—load of botany courses in order to qualify for the doctoral program in that subject, and approved my graduation in Philosophy for May 1975. Due to the fact that the philosophy department did not follow the standard operating procedures of the University, but coerced me to write further drafts for each of Dr. Carson's changes of mind, I was unable to do justice to my courses, and changed them to audits.

After following Dean Strand's advice and suffering through a prejudiced and maladroit Academic Hearing Board, I again followed his advice and tried to please my committee. When I was told by the members that they would require two more typewritten drafts, I dropped out of summer school. In August I changed my major to unclassified, being unable to qualify in Botany, although I continued the classes. In September, I asked Dean Strand if there was a way that I could avoid the contradictory whims of my committee. He said there was, and arranged to have it sent to external referees.

Moon: That was my advice also, Walter.

Garnet: Karl?

Strand: Yes, I did say something on that order. Don't quote me on this, but this whole thing is absurd. I said it might have to be sent out to be decided.

Cant: It will be. Meanwhile, the committee just keeps recommending changes. Anyway, then I began typing for the final draft and hired a typist, again. I changed my courses in Botany to audits again to devote full time to humoring authorities and preparing the manuscript. I gave the prepared script to my typist on September 23. On October 14 I received a memo from Dean Strand stating that he would not send it out until Spring semester, when I would have to change my major back to philosophy and register for courses, apparently any courses, and hopefully I might be finished by May 1976.

Garnet: Karl?

Strand: It cannot be done this semester.

Cant: On October 18, the final draft of the thesis was finished. I have been writing drafts to fulfill my thesis requirement since June 1974. Somewhere in the confusing straits between the Charybdis of the philosophy department, where my thesis has never been read completely and the Scylla of the graduate school, with its alternating procrustean passion for strict rules—

Garnet: Spare the mixed mythology. I get the idea. The rules are necessary for the university degree to have meaning.

Cant: Not these modern rules that hold sway here: The thesis must perfectly reflect the prejudices and limits of the major professor, as well as the standards and mediocrity of the university. It must be dull and not original. It must be fashionable, that is current, and not in advance of anyone, especially tenured persons. It must contain misspellings—

Garnet: Very amusing.

Cant: The Graduate School changes the standards for the thesis and graduation, and the philosophy department and the graduate school seem to have lost their scholarly perspective; so much so, that in their eagerness to prevent one student from receiving a Master's degree, they are willing to violate not only the spirit of the university, but even other faculty rules and the ethics of the community.

According to the *University Handbook*, this university aspires to "imbue the human mind with knowledge, tolerance and vision, and to stimulate a lasting attitude of inquiry." (1100-A)

Strand: We all know the Handbook, okay. Hunter and I wrote part of the new edition. ...

Moon: (I grow weary. Nature amuses us for a moment with the silly bauble of life, then lulls us to forgetful sleep.)

Cant: In my case, however, the University has attempted to shackle a mind with dilettantism, narrowness, and blind obedience, and forcibly install a thoughtless reverence for arbitrary regulations. After the Academic Hearing Board appeal had been denied, my professors felt that I had betrayed and attacked them — Professor Finn called me a 'dog that bit the very hand that fed it.' I am actually grateful for the comparison, for one reason because Immanuel Kant was always being called a 'dog' by clergymen or theologians who disagreed with his treatment of God as an unsolvable riddle. Though the case was denied, it accomplished one end—my committee began to assume hitherto neglected responsibilities, at least briefly, for a while.

Garnet: Is that true? That they never met before now?

Cant: Yes. And in spite of the fact that my appeal was legitimate and supported, the committee resented it and began acting even more contradictorily, in violation of University laws and ethics. Since I have previously illustrated their neglect of procedure, I will offer examples, from bursting possibilities, of how they abused their privileges as faculty, of how they were inefficient in, or unqualified in, their field, and of their libelous reactions to the situation.

Garnet: All right. I trust you have proof.

## The Thesis

Cant: Ample proof, in writing, their handwriting. According to the bylaws of the faculty of the graduate school, a member of the graduate faculty has the privilege, not only to be on a committee, but also to "serve as major professor for graduate students working toward advanced degrees within the faculty member's field or level of competence." (2050-II-3) I think they—

Garnet: Please forego the formality.

Moon: (I was thinking about her again, her perfect shape, not too big or too small, but always lost under the 1940s clothes she wore. I saw her shape once when she was dressing—the mirror on the door. Her back was perfect, shapely, not like the popsicle shape backs many women have; hers curved down from the shoulders ... enough daydreaming. I shouldn't do this. I married Thor for camouflage here in Idahum, but women are so much nicer to look at.)

Cant: —have abused their privilege, for whatever reasons. Ms. Carson has used her position as my major professor to attempt to dictate her own personal style—Webster's Third International, definition 2a—going so far as to change every semicolon to a period, whether or not it is appropriate, and to impose her own procrustean rules—lately, she has decided to limit both the length of the thesis and the quotes within it, citing as her reason her age—31—and her tired eyes.

Moon: Perhaps it is time to retire all professors over thirty.

Strand: Really? She said that? I'm sorry I missed the appeal.

Cant: Yes. She also confessed to wanting to work here always, forever, if you will have her.

Strand: Don't quote me on this, but maybe she's been working too hard.

Cant: Mr. Finn has used his position to exercise his desire to manipulate a student for no other purpose than manipulation, requiring pointless rewrites of his own material, while reinstating what was previously discarded. He limited himself to reading only five pages of more than 1100 pages claiming that they were not ready, or that he was ignorant of the topic.

Strand: That's true. He told me he'd only been able to manage three pages, because it was so incoherent.

Cant: Would either of you be willing to read it?

Garnet: I'll pass for now. Go ahead and finish your argument.

Cant: Mr. Kraft also refused, or could not find the time, to read and comment on any of the first seven drafts. In his statements since the AHB appeal, he has chosen to fault me for not following rules I've already followed, that I tried to get them to follow, or were made up after the fact. For instance, for months, he accepted or asked for either xeroxed pieces or complete xeroxed copies of the seven drafts, but eight months later complained of receiving them piecemeal, and ten months later formulated a policy, to replace the laissez-faire attitude of the philosophy department, with their enthusiastic consent, toward outlawing xeroxed copies being given simultaneously to each member of the committee, and then judging me guilty of violating it, after the fact. That's ridiculous! I have been suggesting the adoption of a formal path for months. Now they claim credit for it and want me to follow what I had suggested to them.

Furthermore, I now think they are inefficient, or unqualified, in their field. Professor Carson exhibited a casual lack of direction, forestalling committee meetings, allowing his student to assume the responsibility of notifying the committee members, ignoring notes and corrections, and misreading the thesis. He was unable even to decide on the form of the thesis, first encouraging prose; then, ignoring poetry, but suggesting aphorisms, then wavering between. After the 4th draft on 1 February 1975, for instance, he offered a choice: "Either Wittgenstein format. Or a conventional thesis with conventional form..." After receiving the 5th draft in mid-February, he decided that the aphorisms were too prosaic: "I regret now that I encouraged you on the Wittgensteinian format, because this draft certainly doesn't fit it." On the 6th draft, 1 March 1974, he found the prose unfortunately too poetic: "too poetic not straight-forward thesis that we need." Finally settling on prose, and finding it tolerable in the 7th draft on March 30th, he gave permission for the final draft and to hire a typist. His comments were specifically for the typist: "read for typist—single-space quotes, etc." He ended his comments with a written echo of his verbal promise: "I think I'm ready to sign this after I talk to Sam and Ronn."

After talking to them, she reversed his decision. Professor Carson also had trouble deciding on the content of the thesis, first instructing me to build it up, then telling me to cut it down. On the 6th draft, for instance, she not only stated: "Salvage Chaps. 10, 12, beginning 13, 14. This should be your thesis," but on the same draft (1 March 1975), she wrote: "Summary comments rewrite thesis using Chapts. 10, 12, 13, 15. 15 reads well..." For the 7th draft I cut out three chapters —9, 16, 17—and asked if I could just rework the remaining ones, i.e., the Introduction and ones on Being." Does this sound like someone who had a clear idea of what the thesis should look like?

Garnet: Do you have those instructions?

Cant: Yes, but not with me. I'll send you copies. Professor Carson said that I could rework some of the chapters to be cut, and I did. She then repeated his comments on the 7th draft and repeated before the AHB, even offering to accept them as the thesis with minimum rewriting. After it was typed, and she read the same draft in June, she appended these contradictory comments: "Cut entirely Chapters on linguistics, Chaps. 10, 11, and 13. Reduce considerably Ch 15." This contradicts what she agreed to in the AHB. Also, after the AHB appeal, where she had said this about the 7th draft: "Some problems... but essentially OKAY..." (June 16th). Then, on July 16th she announced: "The draft we have does not qualify as *complete*."

The background to the whole thing is interesting. Professor Carson began

## The Thesis

reading Merleau-Ponty at the same time I did — our mutual interest grew up together; unfortunately Professor Carson's died first, and she did not read Merleau-Ponty's later philosophy. As an example, on page 18 of the 7th draft I wrote: "Being as being is the perceptible world..." and Professor Carson wrote above that: "this goes against M-P + Heidegger Being is formal (hidden) never identified with beings" I was paraphrasing Merleau-Ponty, who wrote on page 170 of The Visible and the Invisible: "Being - perceived world." This type of thing is not scholarly disagreement, but disagreeable ignorance on Dr. Carson's part. There are other instances with the philosophies of Heidegger and Husserl. For example, when I stated that Heidegger even tried poetic form himself, Dr. Carson said that was "never true." I had to show her the book were Heidegger did this. Dr. Carson has presumed to correct the English in the thesis as well, but she is mistaken even in the errors she points out, in syntax and run-on sentences; examples are on pages 36, 136, and 211.

Mr. Finn's lack of direction is also painfully clear. He held no definite direction for the thesis or for the department's part in producing it. He willfully remained ignorant on the topic; when something in the 7th draft confused him, he wrote 'confused' on that page, and embellished it with floating question marks. I could not abate his confusion with facts.

Mr. Kraft's ignorance of both the subject and English grammar is 2nd to none. He never made original comments, just seconded Finn's and Carson's. For whatever reasons, the actions of the professors on my committee fall short of the minimum standards of the University. The Handbook records that "Professors—

Strand: Not the Handbook again.

Cant: I need the notes to collect my thoughts. —"guided by a deep conviction of the worth and dignity of the advancement of knowledge, recognize the special responsibilities placed upon them .... They practice intellectual honesty." (4220-A) But these professors have successfully resisted responsibility, and certainly have not practiced intellectual or emotional honesty.

For example, Dr. Carson, on the 4th draft, wrote that I didn't need to quote her; on the 5th draft she penciled in that I didn't need to even reference her in the bibliography or even attribute it to her. In commenting on the 7th before the AHB and afterwards she accused me of plagiarizing her statements. Professors Finn and Kraft broke their promises to sign the thesis, unread, when Dr. Carson was ready to do so.

Garnet: Walter, please, where is this leading?

Cant: I'm being penalized, and brutalized, because I challenged them. They are lying about what I did. According to the section in the University Handbook—sorry—on Faculty Professional Ethics, "As teachers, professors encourage the free pursuit of learning in their students. They hold before them the best scholarly standards of their discipline. The demonstrate respect for the student as an individual, and adhere to their proper role as intellectual guide and counselor." (4220-B)

My professors have not respected me, or guided or counseled me. If I was given no direction, and pursued my own interests, then they formed limits and faulted me for violating them. Indeed, these professors have conspired to discredit me. As one instance, after Dr. Finn's secretaries typed most of the 7th draft in June, it was given to Ms. Carson, without being proofread. When Dr. Finn asked for a copy so he could continue mutilating the first 5 pages, I told him that Dr. Carson had it. Apparently he went to Dr. Carson and Xeroxed a copy, as Dr. Carson informed me herself in a note dated June 15th: "P.S. Finn has Chap. One." Afterwards I offered Mr. Kraft the same opportunity, saying only that Mr. Finn had a Xeroxed copy and that he could avail himself if he so desired. In a surprisingly long and repetitious letter Mr. Kraft formed his policy for the philosophy department—quite similar to my earlier recommendations—and admonished me for violating it, stating that Dr. Carson "was however a little shocked to hear that you had given Caesar Sam Finn part of your thesis." (July 11th) This is ridiculous, of course, since I didn't even have it. Contradictorily, later in that same letter he accepts that action as being appropriate: "Finally, in answer to your memo, both Sam and Leigh have advised me that they are currently reading your thesis draft..." and that he would get it afterwards.

Garnet: Walter, please wrap it up, soon.

Moon: (I would have thought that it was bad enough that Carson and Finn might have had knowledge without charity, truly a demonic theme—the word demon even came from the Greek word for knowledge—but the evidence indicates that they had only ignorance without charity. Perhaps that made them sub-demons. They certainly had been exercising power without charity. Knowledge, or power, should always be tempered with charity, for professors and politicians to be more than demons. Was I moralizing? Imagine that—I must be getting tired of this.)

Cant: In writing letters for other persons, for inclusion in my graduate file, and in speaking and writing about me, they have breached the University's code of ethics as well as the common laws regarding slander and libel. Before others, on tape before the AHB, and on paper, Professors Finn, Carson, and Kraft have defamed my character and injured my reputation. They have irrevocably compromised themselves in calling me a plagiarist, a liar, and incoherent, in accusing me of playing games and deceiving them, in stating that I am dishonest, untrustworthy, and in need of psychiatric help. I want all that defamatory material removed from my files.

Garnet: Are they in the Graduate School files?

Strand: If they are, as Walter says they are, the ones that are inappropriate will be removed immediately. I will need a list from you, Walter, of all the files you object to. Then I will decide which ones are to be removed.

Garnet: That will be satisfactory?

## The Thesis

Cant: Eminently. Thank you. Furthermore, throughout the past year, I have been blamed when they did not follow the standard procedures of the University, I have been punished by their misuse of academic privilege, I have suffered for their lack of competence in my area, and I have been injured by their unethical and illegal behavior. I am appealing to you, as the head of the University, to correct this situation — the regular route has failed. With the sudden actions of Dean Strand, the goals of the University seem to be lost in the rush of rules.

Strand: I resent that. What sudden actions? I have been consistent in my recommendations ever since ... well, whenever.

Cant: I'm sorry, but I think you have wavered. In the comic shuffling of personalities and prejudices the question of—

Moon (whispering): Walter, these guys are on your side, if you don't screw it up by insulting them.

Cant: I'm sorry if I have been rude or inconsiderate, but whether or not I have earned or deserve a degree seems to have been shunted aside. I believe that I have, by most standards, fulfilled the requirements for a Master's in philosophy. Therefore I would like to receive it before November 1st, or at least have the final draft sent out, as originally suggested by Dean Strand.

Strand: It can't be done before spring semester, as I said earlier. If you make arbitrary deadlines, you may hang yourself on them.

Garnet: It may be that your knowledge is in advance of your professors on this criminology, I mean phenomenology of, umm, those thinkers. That is often common in graduate school. It is expected in better students. Professors should be proud to have catapulted their students beyond them. Not all perhaps. And it may be that you have been led astray where the rules for completion are ambiguous. The obstacles for your finishing a Masters here are not insurmountable. The Dean has suggested such a path to finish and I strongly recommend that you follow it. I am sympathetic to your plight. It reminds me of a situation, when I was at school at Harvard. Ms. Wilsetten, Wohlstetter, I think, finished her dissertation in Literature; her interpretation of something contradicted her professor's prejudices. He told her to change her interpretation. She refused and withdrew. Fortunately, her book won a Bancroft prize and she became a well-known analyst for the government. I know of several other horror stories that did not turn out as well for the student. Just don't violate your own integrity for the cheap satisfaction of accusing your professors of illegal activities. I hope you get the degree.

Moon: Wittgenstein reminds us that science, and I presume academic fundamentalism, leaves the problems of life 'completely untouched.'

## 20 Culture

I felt after that meeting, the least I could do was treat Ellsin to lunch, so I suggested my favorite hamburger joint, but she countered with the student union, which was also being revamped with blue carpet. So, we walked down hill. I thanked her for participating in this charade, this, whatever experience that goes on forever.

"Maybe a marathon is the word you are looking for, although the first runner died at the end, remember? Don't torture yourself. Partly, it's just our culture, mixed and confused—"

"What do you want to eat?"

"Let's go sit in the student section. It will be noisier and more lively, although the conversations will probably revolve around football."

"Okay, I'm going to cheat and get a hamburger."

"How is the vegetarian diet working out?"

"I eat too much candy. I don't know what it is? Some missing form of protein. Want fries?"

"You're paying? Yes, but I think I'll get the salad bar, too. Thank you by the way."

"Thank you for listening."

"Are you kidding? The entertainment value of this saga is measureless! I haven't had this much excitement since I gave a bad review to Vonnegut. Of course, I'm glad it's your rump in the ringer and not mine."

"What did you mean about culture?" We had been able to gather our food on the trays and navigate through the mostly empty tables, before settling on a large one by the wall, looking outside at the street. "Isn't real culture just knowledge of a few dead languages and a few dead authors? I mean I have culture because I took Latin and Greek and then read the authors in their language."

"One problem is that culture is associated with the best. Matthew Arnold defined culture as the 'acquainting ourselves with the best that has been known and said in the world.' This is almost a global definition of elite culture and it is very value-laden. It means most people have no culture"

"No wonder that what's his name said when he heard the word culture, he reached for his gun."

"That's a normal and understandable reaction. And when I hear talk about God, I reach for my the lid on my bottle of aspirin. By the way, the words were actually: 'When I hear the word culture, I release the safety on my Browning.' Hanns Johst put that in his play *Schlageter*, in 1933. Johst was a good Nazi who hated culture as a fraud that implied liberalism and enlightenment, the cheap talk of weaklings, the Jews and the effete Elite. I wonder if Spiro Agnew ever read that play—never mind. This entire decade has been exciting politically, although maybe not musically."

"Remember when Snow distinguished two cultures in academia: Mathematics and sciences versus the humanities."

"More like subcultures, but academia is a subculture, insulated from the mainstream, although corporations and businesses are sniffing around and may start sponsoring special programs."

"Like McDonalds?"

"Another Mac, Dwight MacDonald said that mainstream culture is mass culture, when it is formed for mass consumption, like chewing gum. There may be a danger. Mass entertainment was described by DH Lawrence described the mass entertainment as 'anti-life' or pro-thing. Our vaunted progress is just the acquisition of things."

"Maybe we should distinguish that culture from the anthropological meaning, where culture is the nongenetic transmission of information. Scientists found that ape behavior can be more sophisticated in human situations, and they claim the sophisticated apes have become enculturated with human culture. But, apes are born imitators and they use that in ape societies."

"Excellent point. And, imitation is emulation, or perhaps fashion, which was the word used by Wolfgang Kohler, who observed apes inventing new games in the early 1920s."

"So, culture exists on many levels and expands historically. Think about how fast information is expanding. With the new computers even here at IMU, we keep concentrating information. I heard that in the entire world now we might have 2 petabytes—that's over a trillion books."

"A petabyte is how many kilobytes?"

"Not sure. Think it's a billion megabytes. How much info do you suppose we had in 12,000 BC or 0 BC or 1400 AD? In all the scrolls or native stories and myths?"

"And, how much will we have in 25 years, I wonder? I just read an interesting number. In the 1930s, 9 of 10 words a person heard were spoken directly, one to one, mouth to ear. By middle of this decade, the proportion was reversed; 9 of 10 came out of an electronic speaker. Computers are already accustoming us to taking orders from electronics."

"Should we put computers in the list of dangers from droughts and earthquakes to conquest and war, then?" I added a little more mustard to the last bite of my burger, thrilled with the secret binge.

"Ironically, that is one theory about why culture formed in humans. It was an adaptation to hardships caused by climates and better predators."

"Yea, but it sure has screwed up with modern threats, like obesity, heart disease, and addictions. It didn't adapt by helping us change our behavior, it just provided chemicals, drugs, and emergency treatments and surgeries. We should be eating less and exercising more, in a healthy environment, not perfectly disease-free, but satisfactorily disease-limited. Has culture reached its limits? Or can we change culture consciously?"

"I agree with you; cultures need to change patterns, local and global. This includes reducing populations, based on requirements for healthy ecosystems, which have full complements of animals, plants and microorganisms."

"I was just sketching out how we need to be restoring or modifying an optimal coverage of wild environments."

"You have mustard on your sleeve. I hate to be a drag, but wage-slavery beckons. Come by tomorrow on your break, so we can continue this conversation. Oh, and thanks again for the gourmet grub."

Gina Painting in the Kitchen

## 21 Driving Around

We had dinner with her parents, Peggy and Philo. Philo was a Professor of Pushups and Physical Education at the university; he was hearty and enthusiastic; the only thing of his that Gina had inherited was the shape of her nose. Peggy was a housewife who kept a beautiful garden, and barely controlled a house with 5 dogs, two horses, a cow, and at least 6 cats. They lived on 50 acres out of town. I couldn't tell if she inherited anything from her mother, who had mousy blonde hair and a retiring, or broken, disposition. The conversation wavered between sports politics and the ladies club. Nevertheless the dinner was very good. On the way back to town, I accidentally mentioned my desire to give up the quest for the brass ring.

"What do you mean you're quitting? You can't. You've worked too hard—"

"But. I don't care—"

"Don't interrupt me. You can't give in to them."

"But, I'm just here to learn, and I learned.

"You're in a degree program. You did the work. You need the degree. How will you get a job? Without a degree?"

"I have a job, without a degree."

"You work in the library.

"As do you."

"Bastard, I am not happy. I want more than that. I want to be a publisher, an artist. I want fame."

I didn't reply, trying to concentrate on keeping the car on the road, instead of aiming it for a handy tree.

"You're a loser. You'll always be a loser."

"Okay, what would you do?"

"I'd appeal to the faculty again. Have someone else look at it."

"A committee? Again?"

"If you want the degree."

"I'm not sure it's worth it …" and I trailed off, thinking that I was wasting my time trying to prove what I already knew—that I had learned a phenomenal lot about phenomenology.

"You're afraid of commitment."

"That's silly. I wanted to get married, not you."

"That's cause I was married, to Barlow. I didn't, don't want that. I want a career, and not as an appendage to some male ego! And I was referring to your inability to complete a course of study."

## 22 A Sad Tale Sent to the Ancient Titans

3 November 1975

Board of Regents:
I am a graduate student at Idaho Modern University. In this letter I would like to outline certain unwarranted actions by University faculty and administration, and then question how these actions could have happened

This is what transpired. I began doing graduate work in the philosophy department at the University in June 1973, paying my tuition from salaries as a part-time teaching assistant in philosophy and as a library clerk. I worked diligently, abided by the rules and regulations of the university, and earned, I hope, the respect of my professors. Unfortunately after I began work on my thesis in June 1974, my Masters Committee, composed of Professors Carson, Finn and Kraft, disregarded the standard University procedure for guiding a thesis.

Professor Carson pressured me into writing 7 drafts in 11 months, advising arbitrary changes in style and content and without having read any of them well. Professors Finn and Kraft refused to read any of the drafts. Professor Finn's ability to crank out criticisms of a thesis he did not read is reminiscent of Jonathan Swift's Professor of Eloquence, who was able to crank out scholarly works automatically with a machine without having knowledge. The committee approved the 7th draft for final typing but reversed their decision after 6 hours. When I protested at last, and was supported by Dean Strand, an Academic Hearing Board was belatedly convened. The AHB, exhibiting hebetude of their own responsibility, refusing to follow the university's rules of order, violating their own impartiality, reached its warped conclusion 3 days after commencement.

In spite of the fact that the appeal was denied, my committee was so vengeful, that to punish my effrontery, they subjected me to considerable abuse. They called me names—"liar," "charlatan," "plagiarist," "dog," as well as repeatedly branding me as "incoherent" and "incompetent." They intentionally interfered with my right to a good name by uttering and publishing messages that lowered my esteem in the academic community. Professor Finn judged that I was in need of psychological counseling. while Professor Carson stated that I was psychologically and emotionally unstable and immature, while Professor Kraft contented himself with falsely accusing me of playing games. Some of this defamation was introduced into my graduate file and the University Archives. These professors maliciously conspired to discredit me by, for example, circulating part of the 7th draft among themselves, spontaneously inventing regulations against such actions, and then blaming me for violating the regulations, while being shocked at the invented violation. At their own request,

## The Thesis

and on Dean Strand's advice, I resubmitted the 7th draft, retyped. When all of the Committee finally read parts of that draft, their uncoordinated comments displayed a shallow understanding of philosophy, while their erroneous correction the style of the thesis revealed an unpardonable ignorance of basic English grammar. Their academic evaluation of my work, when it occurred at all was arbitrary, capricious, and manifestly unjust. Furthermore, after their first and only meeting as a committee, subsequent to their reading, they directly contravened their previous agreement to accept parts of the 7th draft as the final draft, and ordered 2 more drafts for fulfillment of the thesis requirement.

When I presented the situation to Dean Strand, and offered to support my contentions, he characterized it as being absurd, and agreed to my request to send the thesis to competent referees. He then obtained the committee's permission for this action, and authorized me to have the final draft typed. However, the day before the typist finished, Dean Strand sent me a note in which he reversed his decision, stating as a reason my change of major from philosophy to ecology. Indeed, I had been attempting to take ecology courses since January. Dear, Strand directed me to immediately re-enroll in philosophy and resubmit the authorized final draft to the same irresponsible Committee, as a preliminary rough draft.

I was so distressed that I immediately appealed to President Garnet, who sympathetically indicated that it was his understanding, from closely following the correspondence, that the obstacles were not insurmountable, that my knowledge was apparently in advance of my professors, and that he would personally ask the Dean to send the thesis out for assessment. Today, 3 November 1975, I received Dr. Garnet's letter, in which he lamely admits that he was unable to assess the source our distress, and suggested that, according to the rules, there is a quite specific procedure to follow: Dean Strand's 2nd antithetical plan of resubmitting the final draft to the some nescient committee as a rough draft. The administration's contrariety and its vacuous insistence on circular movement renders its decisions meaningless. The committee is obviously unable to comprehend the thesis, much less criticize it. Dr. Strand and Dr. Garnet show pococurantic lack of responsibility, and unwillingness to direct or criticize their faculty. The university, through its interminable political process has arbitrarily refused to confer a demonstrably earned degree.

How could this have happened? At one time thinkers were driven to desperation and ruin; exercising the intellect was a risk, an act of defiance. Perhaps that was why Cant challenged, "dare to know." Thinkers, such as the *philosophes*, who placed their knowing in a frame of social responsibility, were not associated with a universities because universities were violently inhospitable to the most advanced and critical thought of the times. Thinking is still a risk, even now. Wittgenstein noted that "When you are philosophizing you have to descend into primeval chaos and feel at home there." Although the intellectuals have become the establishment, their squeaky challenges are "get the degree," "secure the grant," and "publish or perish." Their business is career competition, not knowing. Most students who cherish thinking and creating are forced to drop out, and then they are labeled "temperamental or unstable" in Professor. Finn's words.

The avowed goal of modern liberal education is to bring the student to a point beyond which she can educate herself and critically examine her education and its consequences to society. In fact, the purpose of the academy, expressed by Jefferson in his plans for the University of Virginia, was to exercise independent criticism of the church and state. Unfortunately, this ideal has not been found to be acceptable to the church and the state, which fund most of the universities today. Indeed, modern education has reversed the tradition. The modern academic establishment proffers advice and blind support to the church and state.

The source of this reversal is easy to identify: the Morrill Land Grant Act (1862) declared that American Public schools be an integral part of the community and service its needs. The community expresses a need for training and entertaining and the university provides it, cloaked with the prestige of higher learning. Faced with a similar situation in the philosophical past, Socrates questioned the meaning of service to the Athenians — was it to combat them until they became as virtuous as possible, or to be their servant and cater to their desires? Socrates combated Athens, and was offered the cup of Hemlock for their pleasure. The question stands, at Idaho: Does one learn, or please one's teachers? The administration and the faculty choose to be catered to.

The educational cacistocracy has strayed from the Greek ideal of rational persuasion, but not from the Greek practice of conformity. Society exerts a tremendous pressure toward uniformity and conventionality. To be an academic has always meant to be "safe," from the viewpoint of civil authorities, and hence petty and irrelevant in the view of thinkers. Contemporary academia can claim the pedigree of this ignoble tradition. The university is a social club that trains the functionaries of tomorrow. Technicians wire students to take their plug-in places in the static world-as-it-is. The university becomes an emporium of marketable skills, a service station on the route to success. And the student purchases his passport to this mechanical utopia with obedience.

Graduate school should force the student to reflect on the function and purpose of her professional commitment, but it doesn't. It results in insouciant specialization and irrelevant pedantry, all clothed in respectability. Professors hide in their professional context, with its training, habits, and allegiance. As scholars they belong to their department, a locus in the network of the community of scholars. Belonging to one profession, philosophers for instance, they forfeit the operation of the university to other professionals, who, in turn leave the departmental autonomy unchallenged—the university becomes a hydra-headed monster with a hundred uncoordinated directions. A graduate student who enters the department becomes part of the community and is expected to play by the rules of the profession. In the philosophy department, the relation of students to faculty is one of subjection, tempered with a joviality and camaraderie that can be stripped off like dirty sheets, revealing the procrustean iron bed. To keep the bed made, the student must offer acceptable tokens; for instance, on a test, many professors expect to receive only the information given out, not what else may have been learned. Professor Finn once awarded me a D- on a test because the information was not phrased the way he phrased it in class, although the answers were correct and comparable with any A paper. If the student is to get a degree, find a job, and home in suburbia, he must be obedient to the powers that control the rewards. And when they are achieved, the student may then enforce the same expectations on her apprentices when she sponsors them for the guild of crafters of philosophies. All that is lost in the orthodox dogma is scholarship and originality.

The evolution of Professor Carson from enthusiastic thinker to departmental martinet is illustrious of this process. The intellect is degraded to a means of career building, when so clipped by conformity. Our professors ask us to ponder Socrates, Spinoza, and Kierkegaard, who fought to dignify the life of the mind, but what do these examples mean to them? Do my professors cultivate and defend the values of civilization or do they make themselves comfortable like hotel managers at a convention? Wittgenstein said, "A philosopher gets into the position of an incompetent manager who, instead of getting on with his own work and just keeping an eye on his employees to make sure they do theirs properly, takes over their work until one day he finds himself overloaded with other people's work, while his employees look on and criticize him."

Professor Carson teaches Heidegger, but is herself inauthentic; Professor Finn teaches Socrates, but he refuses to examine his own life; Mr. Kraft demonstrates ceramics, but he cannot shape himself into an original. Their failure is not completely their fault, but is a standard inadequacy of education. Professors ostensibly give themselves over to the life of the mind, but pathetically plead their powerlessness to reform, or even attempt to reform, the academic wasteland. Their accomplishments are just sufficient to give reasons for abandoning their intellectual responsibilities. As C. Wright Mills so appropriately stated, "They use the liberal rhetoric to cover the conservative default."

I cannot blame my committee for failing to indoctrinate me; the very structure of the university requires them to prevent change in any deep and significant way. Indeed, my professors are not even culprits, but valiant slaves, condemned by their lack of imagination or courage to perpetuate the system that enslaves them. I do not blame the administration for their floundering tergiversation in the morass of rules; they only lack concern and logic. To pervert Santayana's image, they sit in a smiling garden, and blindly fashion paper flowers with fastidious skill. I know the security of busy work, and I am tempted by it. I want my degree, even if it is in this case a trivial recognition of conformity. Now that I have been defamed and ostracized, I will accomplish what I can, as a poet and philosophe, whose very citizenship is an ethical vocation. I no longer care if I get the degree, only that I can continue to learn, I will not fight the University, but I will help it— against its will in a good Socratic fashion —to be a better university. The University must approach the spirit of its own goals and not just enforce the letter of its rules in a whimsical retaliation against the questioning of the rules. The social relevance of learning should be an integral part of education. Education must include criticizing, exposing, questioning, resisting, and dissenting, as well as praising, supporting, and clarifying. The dichotomous occupational disease between thinking and doing must be cured at an existential level: Knowledge must be applied to be wisdom.

Sincerely,
Walter Cant

## 23 Imitation

In the Lobby of the new brick Law School, we were standing watching the faculty arrive.

"Notice how faculty members imitate each other? Notice the coats. If one sees a movie with an English professor wearing a grey herringbone coat with leather patches, pretty soon all of them are wearing it. Or a pipe. Or when one of them stops wearing ties, then they all will stop."

"That's because they are vertebrates and have a unique capacity: imitation. Imitation permits a mode of interaction to goes beyond the limits of an individual."

"What makes you think these creatures have a spine?"

"Imitation, or copying behavior is a drive that reinforces itself. Chimpanzees, for instance, learn to crack open oil-palm nuts using tools. This may start with the young copying the mother's behavior, to be like her or to please her to strengthen the mother-infant bond. They may have to practice for three years to be able to coordinate hitting nuts with one stone as an anvil and another as a hammer. This nut-breaking is most often done at the end of the fruit season, when fruits are not available. They can get nine times the kilocalories that they put in as effort. That's a good return. Tool technology is a critical skill for eating and maintaining health. Stones are often kept at the nut 'factory' although mothers may move the stones to familiarize infants with them. Imitation, maybe like automatic education, helps them survive certain environmental conditions."

"Yes, well put. It is reinforced because it shifts from identity with the mother to getting rewards, that is, food. However, most behavior does not change for a long time, especially in chimps, apes, and professors, but, then culture is conservative and has inertia as well as some occasional innovation."

"Culture again. If culture solves problems, then what does human fashion have to do with problems? Are leather elbow patches more meaningful or adaptive? What about religion, food preferences, art, dancing, or social styles of politeness?"

"One popular idea is that biology restricts our freedom, but culture frees us from biology. On the other hand, the capacity for culture rises from biology. Furthermore, culture can restrict freedom as much as biology. Notice that none of the profs is wearing a meter-long, decorated penis shaft or has a facial tattoo. Our culture regards these as meaningless."

"We have a culture? No, wait! I know, there is an IMU subculture of the dominant industrial culture."

"I was just thinking that culture in chimps requires more than a personal perspective. One had to understand that the other is also an individual with needs. Hand-clasping, during mutual grooming, is observed by the young and it can be taught by the mothers. Teaching transmits acceptable forms of social behavior. You might find a lesson there for yourself."

"What? That I should wear herringbone and adopt a bored neutral facial expression? That I should follow orders and never let my ideas stray from the stale fascism of academia?"

"That would be a start. We'd better go in or they make some decision without us. This is a school of law, so no cussing or spitting on the floor."

"I just want it to be over. I'm trying to finish a portrait."

"Oh, how renaissance. Let me see it someday."

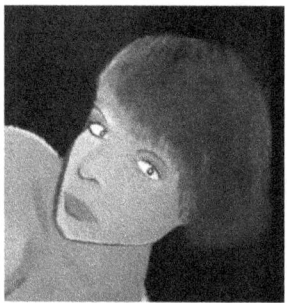

Walter's Portrait of Gina on the Couch

## 24 Standing before the Seated Faculty Council

May 10, 1976

We have assembled in a meeting room in the brand new law school, a brick box across the street from the library. The room had brick walls and a low, white-spray ceiling. The table was large and new with cheap wood veneer. The chairs were hideously uncomfortable plastic molds, obviously designed for the narrower hips of men; my legs would go to sleep after ten minutes and I would have to sit forward on the edge. Walter was frowning.

I asked him: "So, what happened in your meeting with Strand last month?" I hadn't seen Walter much. I assumed he was working on his new courses in Biology still and had let the thesis slide.

"He said it might go out in the summer. That's why I asked for this hearing. To try to force some action. Shit. I'll be appealing my dissertation in Biology before this philosophy thing ever ends." He might have said more, but the Ad Hoc committee had assembled.

"Good morning, my name is Glasgot Duran. I'm the Chairman of this Faculty Ad Hoc Appeal Committee and a Professor of Law. I note that Mr. Cant, Profs. Finn, Carson, and Kraft are here. Are you Ellsin Moon, Mr. Cant's counsel?"

"I am Ellsin Moon, Mr. Cant's witness," I answered. My, this hearing was certainly more formal. I wonder if they were doing this just for Walter; maybe it was going to be a trial. Duran was a thin man with the nervous mannerisms of an ex-smoker longing for a cig. He continued.

"On January 20th, 1976, the Faculty Council appointed an Appeal committee consisting of Larson J. Cohn, D. Wally Ekerd and myself to act for it in the appeal of Walter Cant to the Faculty Council of the Academic Hearing Board regarding his masters degree thesis. The function of this committee is to review the actions of the AHB. It is not the function of this committee to conduct a new evidentiary hearing. We have reviewed the transcript of the case, in April, I believe. Both the petitioner and the respondents had an opportunity to exchange written statements about the operation of the board and to reply to each other's petitions and replies. We will now consider oral argument on whether the AHB followed proper procedures, inquired into the appropriate issues, and whether its findings are supported by the evidence. This committee will follow the following procedures, and I must insist that they be adhered to rigorously. Each side will have 30 minutes to make a presentation. The petitioner will be asked to proceed first, although he may reserve up to 10 minutes of his time for rebuttal after the respondents' oral argument. The purpose of the oral arguments is to allow each side to explain its written arguments and to respond to the questions of the members of the committee. This committee will then meet in executive session to discuss the matter and reach an impartial decision. Mr. Cant, will you make your presentation, now?

Cant: Thank you, Professor Duran. I would like to ask first if my answers to the committee's questions are deducted from my time?

Duran: No, umm, I will say no.

Moon: (Time to find out who is underneath the little martinet. A few deft recombinations and: Duran, what is he? 'ant dog rug' or 'god gun rat' or a 'rotund gag?')

Cant: Thank you. Since I have already answered, in detail, the written statement of their findings on 16 June 1975 in the testimony that follows I shall address myself to evidence presented and the transcription of the tapes. I contend that the AHB made four grievous errors during the hearing: they did not use Robert's Rules Of Order, or any rules of order, as stipulated in the University Handbook; they accepted irrelevant mouthings from Professors Carson, Finn and Kraft; they ignored the admissions of errors by Carson, Kraft and Finn, and they overlooked the conclusive written evidence that I had followed the ambiguous directions of Ms. Carson; finally, they even drew the wrong conclusions from the testimony they did accept.

1. While we were waiting for the tape recorder to arrive, I asked Mr. Dodd to describe the function of the AHB. When he expressed ignorance, I gave him my copy of the appropriate Handbook pages. I asked if the AHB would follow the standard rules of order. He stated that he would prefer an informal hearing. I agreed, with the condition that if exchanges broke down, we would revert to Robert's Rules of Order. The taping began soon after he agreed. After my statement, Professor Dodd defended himself by saying that he set up the hearing board as soon as he was informed of my appeal; this was a curious beginning, since I have his note suggesting that summer school might be more agreeable- a suggestion I not only refused but threatened legal action to avoid. Throughout the length of the appeal, Professor Dodd was unable to maintain order, or direct the proceedings, allowing free argument, general interruptions, and double surrebuttals Please note pages 7, 8, 9, 11, 12, 16, 21, 22, 23, 24, 25, 26, 27, 28, 29, 36, 37, 38, 51, 53, 58, 60, 62, and 63, for example.

2. The AHB accepted irrelevant opinions and defamations of character from Kraft, Carson and Finn. Ms. Carson selected the worst pieces from an *untyped* 4th draft of my thesis, and masqueraded them as being from the 7th draft; this happened at least twice, to the obvious consternation of the AHB. Examples are on pages 11, 12, 25, 26, 27, 28, and others.

Duran: Please be specific Mr. Cant.

Moon: (He's kidding? Duran, Mr. 'gator dung,' he meets up with a 'tudor

# The Thesis

gang' and buys a 'tango drug' so he can see 'god gun art' and then 'nod rug tag' asleep.)

Cant: Ms. Carson claimed that the number of drafts was inflated by one; I disagreed. Regardless, any number over two is inexcusable —agreement is indicated on pages 7, 8, and 11 through 14). Ms. Carson repeatedly aired that I boasted that he would "convince" the others to sign—page 63 et alii. The AHB took that word to heart, over my protests—I had only said that she said it. Mrs. Carson claimed the thesis was too long on pages 9 and 10), but this was misconception on his part; then, Mrs. Carson claimed the quotes were too long on page 10), but had no basis for this, either. Mrs. Carson hammered away at the poor transition between one sentence paragraphs on pages 13 and 21, but this opinion also was a result of his own misunderstanding. Furthermore, Mrs. Carson had approved the theses of the previous two candidates, even though they included longer paragraphs and quotes—

Duran: This is new evidence, Mr. Cant, and cannot be allowed.

Carson: Professor Carson. Yes.

Moon: (That Duran, he's a 'gourd gnat' with 'grand gout' and a 'dragon gut' so mad he'll put the 'gun to grad' and then 'do runt gag.')

Cant: With all due respect, Mr. Chairman, the evidence was referenced on page 59 and offered to the AHB at that time.

Carson: No, it wasn't.

Cant: Are you presuming to know what was in my briefcase? That material which I offered and no one looked at?

Duran: All right, I'll admit it if it seems pertinent.

Cant: I believe it is. Here is an example of a three page paragraph in Romeo's thesis, page 70 to 72, and Rhodes's thesis, pages 82-84. Samples of three-page quotes in Romeo pages 69-72 and Rhodes pages 61-63.

Moon: (Ah, Lana Romeo; I see the 'amoral one' in the library. 'A loon mare,' she likes to 'roam alone' drinking 'maroon ale' trailing her 'lone aroma.' Phew. And Eric Jut Rhodes, 'rude Joe Christ,' I've heard the 'jet ride chorus' and the 'just rider echo' from the 'horrid cue jest' praising 'her justice rod.' So few letters to make so many good little stories.)

Carson: This material should have been sent to us first.

Cant: It was. It's in appendix E. In my case Mrs. Carson writes "sloppy" on a two-page quote and chastises me for having a two-page paragraph, having approved four-page quotes for earlier students. So, you'll note, she has been inconsistent in her treatment of me. The others were not much better. Mr. Finn relaxed us with stories about Aristotle and Wittgenstein, on pages 30 through 36, before offering opinions to the effect that I was difficult to help, on page 36. Mr. Kraft restricted his testimony to a cheap character assassination, making up stories of my divisiveness and game-playing, on pages 11, 12, 18, and 66, and others.

Number 3. The AHB ignored most of the verities in the case, or managed to rationalize them away. Mrs. Carson specifically instructed me to write 6 of the 7 drafts—refer to the written evidence given to AHB.

Mrs. Carson admitted that she encouraged me to write in different forms—pages 8,9.

Mrs. Carson claims that the 4th draft of the thesis was not a draft, just a collection of notes (p. 10); then she admits it is a draft (p. 12); later, she claims that the 4th draft was the essentially conventional thesis she wanted to read (p. 25).

Mrs. Carson falsely identified the 4th draft as the 7th, and said that pages 177-196 were part of it (p. 25); afterwards, she admitted that.

Mr. Carson admitted that *Lebensforms* were difficult to write, and she just wanted to see how I did with them; she also admitted her bad judgment (p.27).

Mrs. Carson admitted that there were no mistakes in the thesis, that her only objection was style (pp. 29, 39). Mrs. Carson's earlier statements indicate that she had no clear conception of what style ought to be (pp.. 3,17).

Mrs. Carson was unable to decide on the form of the thesis: on the 3rd draft she suggested a Wittgensteinian format; after the 4th she offered me a choice; "Either Wittgenstein ... or ... conventional form." After the 5th she said it was "too prosaic" (p.14), and after the 6th she said it was "too poetic" (p.13). The 7th she indicated she would sign (refer to evidence given to AHB).

After she asked me to expand it, Mrs. Carson asked me to cut it down, but she was never able to decide how (pps. 12, 25); on the 6th draft (1 March 1975) she stated, "Salvage Chapts. 10,12, beginning 13,14. This should be your thesis." (AHB evidence) At the end of that same draft she wrote "Summary comments rewrite thesis using Chapts. 10,12,13,15. 15 reads well..." (AHB evidence) For the 7th draft I cut out 3 chapters, 9,16,17, and asked if I could just reduce the rest; she agreed. After reading the 7th she wrote, "Cut entirely Chapts. 10,11 and 13. Reduce considerably Chapter 15." These were most of the same chapters she wanted as the basis of the thesis! (AHB evidence).

Mrs. Carson admitted being unable to find grammatical errors, or improper usages in the 7th draft (p.29); this is in contrast to her earlier claim of incredible misusages throughout (pps. 8, 9, 13) Mrs. Carson tacitly admitted that I had corrected all of his requests on the 7th draft within 2 hours of receipt (p.24)

Mrs. Carson was alarmed that I judged her comments cursory (p.8). Yet she admitted that she overlooked mistakes, and did not read much of it critically (pps. 21, 22).

Mrs. Carson claimed that he approved the Aristotle section because a) it was not of consequence, b) she was confused on Aristotle, and c) she had no direct knowledge of Aristotle (p. 37).

Mrs. Carson claimed that no one could have typed the 7th draft, but Mr. Finn's secretaries were typing it as she spoke; later a final draft was typed from it

# The Thesis

(pp. 9, 14).

Mrs. Carson admitted that her attention span was short and that she was sick and tired of the thesis (p. 52).

Duran: Is this level of detail necessary?
Cant: I'm not sure. But, that is why I had it typed out for you. If I may,

Mrs. Carson admitted approving the thesis, and directing a 3rd of his comments to the typist that she suggested I hire (pps. 14, 65).

Mrs. Carson claimed that Finn and Kraft could **see** that the manuscript of the 7th draft was not ready (p. 22). Mrs. Carson said that she compromised herself by saying she would sign it (p. 65).

Mr. Finn outlined the steps whereby Eric Rhodes finished his thesis: Eric wrote one draft, and sent it to Leigh, who said he rewrote it and circulated it to the other two committee members, who made their comments, and phoned Eric long distance to inform him of their corrections, and that they would sign it, then (p. 29). Contrast that with the tortured treatment of my drafts. Mr. Finn judged that I knew little of Aristotle, not even how to quote him (p. 32), but later admitted that I was always found to be correct in my knowledge of Aristotle (p. 36). Mr. Finn conceded that Leigh's intention to sign my thesis was the same as in Eric's case, but Dr. Finn refused to acknowledge that I had corrected Leigh's suggestions. Mr. Finn admitted that he had only read 6 pages of more than 1100 in 7 drafts, claiming that he didn't need to (pps. 55, 56). Mr. Finn said that his comments on the thesis are like Mr. Kraft' s (p. 55).

Mr. Kraft admitted that maybe he read it wrong (p. 43). Mr. Kraft stated that his comments were ambiguous, and his instructions vague (p. 55). Mr. Kraft admitted reading what he read out of order (p. 44). Mr. Kraft judged the thesis "incoherent" (pps. 42, 66). Mr. Kraft conceded that he did not even **see** the 7th draft (p. 49). Mr. Kraft submitted that the 7th draft was not worthy of a degree (p. 55). Mr. Kraft was unable to 'remember' the topic of the thesis, or even one error in it, or any of his comments about it; he was unable to find any written suggestions; he did not remember meeting, or how many drafts he received. Mr. Kraft stated that I did not follow Mrs. Carson's clear directions. Parenthetically, Mr. Kraft revealed erroneously that **none** of my poetry had ever been published (p. 43). Much of it has been published. Perhaps he meant to say that he had never read any of the journals in which it was published.

I claimed, and offered to prove, that almost all corrections were made on those 6 drafts Mrs. Carson commented on (pps. 28, 29). I submitted all 7 drafts to the AHB, to be examined, and the corrections ascertained; they ignored them. After Mrs. Carson sent arbitrary pieces of an untyped copy of the 2nd draft to members of the AHB, I offered the typed 7th draft a draft Mr. Carson said in December 1974 might be final. Mrs. Carson's comments on this 7th draft consisted of 3 words basically— "cut," "keep" or "expand"— and were all penciled in lightly in Mrs. Carson's handwriting, (all drafts offered after taping, as agreed—p. 26).

The AHB was unable to make a fair decision on the evidence it found acceptable. Mr. Dodd was confused by the 4th draft; he assumed it was relevant evidence, but admitted that it was over his head (p. 12). Mr. Dodd offered to look at the thesis later (p. 26). He never did.

Mr. Sooner was confused by the 7th draft, and requested a recent one (pps. 27, 28). I offered to give him one after the hearing; he declined then to take one. Mr. Sooner questioned the events leading to Mrs. Carson's promise to sign; under rigorous cross-examination, neither Mrs. Carson nor myself were able to remember the exact circumstances other than that he agreed to sign after talking to the Caesar and C. Ronn, and gave me permission to hire a typist (pps. 58-63).

Mr. Holland questioned whether all the instructions were clear; Carson claimed they were, and Finn stated they were faultless (p. 59). Mr. Holland asked if the committee had reached an acceptable level of confidence in the 7th draft, and if it was acceptable in terms of University standards; the committee each said no without reading most or any of it (p. 55).

The AHB condemned me for being out of order in a meeting notable for its disorder. The AHB judged that I had not followed Mrs. Carson's directions, but only by ignoring the indisputable facts presented to them—instead accepting the irrelevant opinions offered by the thesis committee. Somehow, without reading more than a few disjunctive fragments, the AHB determined that I did not make the corrections submitted by Mrs. Carson (or the imaginary ones claimed by Finn and Kraft), without bothering to examine 2 consecutive drafts. In considering Mr. Sooner cross-examinations the AHB was able to conclude that Mrs. Carson's memory was perfect, while mine was fogged by trickery, but only by choosing the "evidence" to fit their prejudice. In order to obscure the unprofessional and unethical behavior of Professors Finn, Carson and Kraft, the AHB—Dodd, Sooner, Holland, and Old—sadly compromised itself with that same behavior.

After the hearing ended, I stayed behind to help pack up the taping equipment. And after the technician left, I gathered up the outline and the various drafts of my thesis that the AHB refused to take in their hurry to leave. I sat for another 20 minutes and then left.

Duran: Is that all? Good. Who is representing the Thesis Committee?

Finn: I am, Mr. Chairman. Although Mr. Cant has included his letter to President Garnet in his letter of March 26, 1976, to the Faculty Council Appeals Committee, we will deal, in the first part of our response, with the more specific letter addressed to the Appeals Committee. In his initial statement, Mr. Cant writes: "In the paragraphs that follow, I shall address myself to the evidence presented and the transcription of the tapes." In the first sentence of his paragraph #1, he states: "While we were waiting for the tape recorder to arrive..." These two sentences are mutually exclusive.

# The Thesis

Cant: No, they are not. The unrecorded conversation is still evidence—
Duran: Mr. Cant, there are to be no inter—
Finn: It is hearsay and not admis—
Duran: Mr.—Professor Finn, please continue.

Finn: Mr. Cant charges that the Academic Hearing Board made four grievous errors. The first of these was that "they did not use *Robert's Rules of Order*, or any rules of order, as stipulated in the University Handbook..." This charge is repeated in Paragraph number 1 where Mr. Cant writes: "I asked if the AHB would follow the standard rules of order. He—Professor Dodd— stated that he would prefer an informal hearing. I agreed, with the condition that if the exchanges broke down, we would revert to *Robert's Rules of Order.*" These claims are not a part of the transcript, and are therefore hearsay. In the transcript we note that Professor Dodd did in fact (p. 1) set up an order of procedure for the hearing. Mr. Cant states, in Paragraph 1, that Professor Dodd was unable to maintain order, allowing interruptions, and other matters to be considered below. Concerning interruptions, *Robert's Rules of Order* do specify "that a person may not speak unless recognized by the chair." Throughout the 66 pages of the transcript, there are a total of 114 interruptions. Mr. Cant made 60 of them.

Moon: (Mr. Finn was a man on whom the Gods had bestowed the gift of perpetual old age. He's acted old ever since he's been at this university. Walter told me that he had his lectures memorized from giving them so often, and that the teaching assistants, of which Walter was one for a year, had to read the lectures word for word. On those rare times when Mr. Finn was in the back of the class, he was able to correct any deviation from the calcified content. Yet, new material confused him. The fact that Walter appealed the thesis confused him.)

Finn: —Appeals Committee may be interested in Mr. Cant's claim in this letter that when asked to describe the function of the Academic Hearing Board, Professor Dodd "expressed ignorance."

Cant: Mr. Finn, that is hearsay, also. I trust it is equal in importance to the information I intro—
Duran: Mr. Cant, you cannot interrupt the respondents.
Cant: Mr. Duran, according to *Robert's Rules of Order*, there are conditions under which it is appropriate for me to interrupt. I can—
Duran: My rules for this procedure supersede Robert's. We will have no interruptions.
Cant: I will agree for the moment.

Finn: If testimony were taken, as I was saying, it would show that Mr. Cant told Mr. Dodd that he hoped the AHB would award him his degree. Mr. Dodd said the AHB could not do this.

Professor Dodd did a good job of keeping-the hearing moving, while at the same time allowing Mr. Cant considerable opportunity to express himself. Going back to the original complaint in paragraph 1, Mr. Cant states:

"Throughout the length of the appeal, Mr. Dodd was unable to maintain order, or direct the proceedings, allowing for argument general interruptions, and double surrebuttals." In the sentence quoted, it is unclear whether the five clauses are meant to be parallel or antithetical, and it is unclear whether 'double surrebuttals" are better or worse than single surrebuttals. By definition, a surrebuttal must come from the plaintiff, so again Mr. Cant seems to be objecting to his own actions. But we do not see why Mr. Cant objects to his being permitted the opportunity for a surrebuttal, whether single or double. As a matter of fact, permitting such surrebuttals would seem to prove that the Hearing Board did its utmost to allow Mr. Cant to present his case.

In his letter of June 15, 1975, addressed to President Garnet, in addition to the above complaint about the conduct of the Hearing, Mr. Cant states, on page 1, lines 6 and 7) that "... the AHB suddenly agreed to meet (so suddenly that my advisor was unable to attend)." This letter was written after the Hearing was held, the, hearing at which Ellsin Moon was present as his advisor or council. Most of the details relevant to setting the date of the hearing—

Moon: Pardon me, but I am not Walter's counsel. His counsel is a third-year law student. I merely tag along as an interested witness.

Duran: Mrs. Moon, ah—

Moon: 'Professor Moon' will do. I believe you made the same mistake in introducing me. Walter is right about Robert's Rules, by the way, as stated in the *Faculty Handbook*. That's all I have to say at the moment.

Finn: —to continue, to dating the set the hearing, umm, they are set forth by Professor Dodd and show that Mr. Cant did not follow proper procedure in seeking a hearing. Furthermore, note Mr. Cant's hearsay evidence that Mr. Dodd wanted to postpone the hearing until summer, and that Mr. Cant threatened legal action if it was. From the evidence of the transcript, as above, Professor Dodd received the request on May 12th and did arrange for it by May 15th; it did not appear that Mr. Cant had grounds for complaint on this score.

Cant: More hearsay? It must be evidence.

Duran: Mr. Cant, for the last time ...

Finn: To move to the realm of hearsay again, we are told by Professor Dodd that after he discovered Mr. Cant wanted a Hearing, he called the members of the Hearing Board and found that he couldn't get a quorum at that time. However, Mr. Cant went directly to Vice President Bono and threatened legal action if the Hearing were not held before the semester ended. Vice President Bono, at Mr. Cant's insistence, directed Professor Dodd to arrange for a Hearing before the semester closed, which by that time he could do. If Mr. Cant did not have sufficient notice to have his advisor present, it was a problem of his own making. The advisor who did appear was the one Mr. Cant told Professor Dodd he wanted at the Hearing.

## The Thesis

Moon: (I cannot believe that the committee is going to count every interruption and answer every sentence. Not in half an hour. What, I could imagine that new secretary for half an hour. Starting at her fingertips and working to the first knuckle, the second, the delicate web between the fingers ...)

Finn: We do not understand how anyone can follow ambiguous directions, or what evidence would prove it, and so consider this part of Mr. Cant's statement an emotional utterance, devoid of content. Concerning errors, Mr. Cant does list a number of instances in which he contends his committee members made errors, but he does not show or attempt to show how the AHB ignored those items.

Cant: Because there's no mention of them. You cannot show that they addressed them, because they did not.

Finn: You cannot show it. As for me, Mr. Finn, not knowing Aristotle, the transcript does not support Mr. Cant's contention that he was always found to be correct in his "knowledge of Aristotle." What it says of Mr. Cant's writing is that "whenever we looked up a quote on Aristotle, it was there." The point is that he uses his quotes out of context.

Moon: Sam, a quote is always out of context, isn't it?

Finn: We note in passing Mr. Cant's habit of judging the decisions and judgments of others according to what he wants to happen. For example in paragraph #2, the following: "Mrs. Carson claimed the thesis was too long (pp.. 9, 10), but this was misconception on his part; then, Mrs. Carson claimed the quotes were too long (p. 10), but had no basis for this, either." Wishful thinking.

Turning now to Mr. Cant's letter to President Garnet of June 16, 1975, the first claim—procedural difficulties, time difficulties, etc.—has been dealt with already in this hearing. Concerning the remainder of Mr. Cant's letter, the statements correctly describing events are so intermingled with misrepresentations and assertions which other persons involved deny, and which the transcript itself refutes, that the claims cannot constitute grounds for reversing the Academic Hearing Board's decision.

Cant: Pardon me, Sam, but isn't that more hearsay?

Finn: Evidentiary hearsay. For example, reference is made in paragraph 3 to "...the monumental aberration from departmental procedures by my committee." A later reference is made to Mr. Finn's statement of the "normal procedures of his department." This is a misrepresentation of the testimony, compare pages 29 and 30, which shows that what Mr. Finn I stated was not the normal procedure of the department, but the extent to which the Department would make exceptions to normal procedures to help any Master's candidate who is willing to accept help, and is trustworthy in following directions.

Cant: And how was that different from normal procedure. Not to rewrite the candidate's thesis?

Carson: You are not a candidate!

Duran: Cant, Carson. Cant, I will censure you.

Cant: Censure is for a personal attack, not a legitimate interruption.

Finn: May I? Again, in paragraph 3, reference is made to "Dr. Carson's definite approval," a claim not support by the transcript. Further, nothing in the transcript supports the claim that Mr. Finn told Dr. Carson he would never read the thesis. No evidence is given that would support the claim that Mr. Finn intended to sign if Carson signed—a claim which is false. Finally, Mr Cant writes: "The AHB notes that I relied on a single sentence of acceptance from Dr. Carson; was more necessary?" Given the number of negative comments on the draft on which the sentence in question occurred, as explained in detail by Professor Carson, note pages 14 through 16—clearly, more was needed.

In less detail, paragraph 4 questions the judgment of the Academic Hearing Board and the integrity of Professor Kraft, without supplying any new evidence. Paragraph 5 questions the judgment of the Academic Hearing Board and veracity and judgment of Professor Carson, again without citing new evidence. In paragraphs 6, 7, 8, 9, 10, and 11, Mr. Cant contends that the judgments of the AHB were not fair and that his statement of facts and interpretation of the significance of these facts should be taken.

Moon: (Finn, anagrams for Finn. Hmm. Damn it now, I forgot where I was on Gina's body. Hope I don't have to speak ... Oh, yes, Finn: 'ms inane fracas' is 'as anemic snarf' as you could find if you were to 'scan fan armies'.)

Finn: Let me mention some more specifics from our appendices on this case. In appendix E, where Cant: says "Immediately after that quote, I took it to Professor Carson and I said, well, I—the reason I can't do this is because the thesis is a coherent whole. And that I can't cut out a simple part of it. But I did reduce it 50 pages." This Statement false; no demonstration made.

Cant: That's a lie! I brought all the copies. You simply refused to acknowledge the reduction, since you never got beyond page 3.

Finn: I'm ignoring you, Walter.

Duran: Good. Shut up, Cant.

Finn: Additional citations show that some alterations were in fact made, but that Mr. Cant's ideas of coherency do not agree with his advisor's. Then Cant says, "I submitted all 7 drafts to the AHB, to be examined, and the corrections ascertained but they ignored them." No citation. However, from the decision of the AHB, p. 2, Ln 14-21: "To buttress this complaint Cant selected some twenty odd pages of objections, suggestions and comments made by Carson at various stages and drafts—

Cant: Another lie! Sam, you saw the drafts. I handed some around. You know the AHB comment referred to Leigh's suggestions only.

Finn: —of—humfh. Carson noted, as did the AHB, that the submissions were extensively clear, specific and consistent so that points and defects to which

## The Thesis

Carson took exception in the early drafts are readily recognizable when the same defects occur in subsequent revisions, including the one Cant claims is finished. Statement false.

Cant: Excuse me, but I believe the transcript will show that at no time were two parts of any draft ever compared—the AHB refused to read anything. They left them on the table after the hearing!

Duran: Mr. Cant, you are now censured. If you keep it up, I will stop the hearing as it stands.

Ekerd: Please let Professor Finn finish.

Moon: (She **is** awake. D—for Diane? Wally—for Wallice? was a round unselfconsciously, unwitting woman in the mold of Shelley Winters playing Lolita's mom. Let's see, moving this letter ... you can see that 'we led darkly')

Cant: Is this committee ready to examine any of the drafts?

Duran: Mr. Cant, we cannot afford to take the time to go into that much detail on just an appeal of a hearing. Surely—

Cant: Sounds familiar, I think.

Finn: As I was saying, in Appendix F section 47, sentence 3, Cant says. "After Mrs. Carson sent arbitrary pieces of an untyped copy of the 4th draft to members of the AHB, I offered the typed 4th draft—a draft Mrs. Carson said in December 1974 might be final. Mrs. Carson's comments on this 4th draft consisted of 3 words basically—cut, keep or expand—and were all penciled in lightly in Mrs. Carson's handwriting (all drafts offered after taping, as agreed-p. 26). No citations for major portion of this. No reference made to 'drafts offered after taping.' Statement confused; citation not applicable; no visible conclusion.

Cant: Do not mistake your confusion for mine or any conscious being. The statement was witnessed, as well as taped.

Duran: Mr. Cant, your, ah, formal rebuttal.

Cant: Thank you. Let's start by looking at the faculty handbook and *Robert's Rules of Order*. The faculty handbook states on page 37 that *Robert's Rules of Order* will be used in all meetings. Please not that evidentiary—the word is evidentiary, not evidencery or evidentious or whatever—appeals are not excluded from application here. The AHB and the thesis committee now maintain that I was out of order. Let us examine if I was. *Robert's Rules of Order*, the 1970 edition, pages 324-5. I quote: "When a member has been assigned the floor ... he cannot be interrupted by another member or by the chair except for one of the following purposes, and only when the urgency of the situation justifies it: a) a Call for the Orders of the Day when not being conformed to; b) the raising of a question of privilege (e.g., if a pressing situation is affecting the right or privilege of an individual member, e.g., introduction of a confidential subject in company)." That's when Leigh should have objected to my introduction of what he said about his bosses.

Carson: I never said bosses!

Cant: What, Mr. Duran, no censure for Leigh? I continue: "e) a request or inquiry that requires an immediate response."

In numerous cases the chair did not call members to order when they questioned the motives of other members or when they spoke on completely irrelevant matters. For instance, Mr. Kraft repeatedly and falsely accused me of trying to play off professors against each other and of introducing errors into the thesis to test those same professors. In this case Mr. Kraft was clearly guilty of a breach of order. The chair should have proposed that he offer an apology or have censured him—this is the proper use of censure, Mr. Duran. Instead the committee chose to make such remarks the centerpiece of their judgment.

Duran: I am so informed.

Cant: After an interruption, which was justified by the behavior of the speaker, the speaker continues to have the floor. The AHB got that part right at least.

When I presented a number of drafts to the AHB the AHB accepted the precedence of that documentation. The ASHB was out of order in reconsidering the number of drafts as deflated by all the members of the Master's committee. The number was not debatable.

Furthermore, the debate itself was not exhausted because not all the questions presented had been addressed or acted on by the AHB. Thus, the AHB was in error there, also.

Reading from reports can only without objection or with permission. Pages 248-9. "If any member objects, a member has no right to read from ... any paper or book." The AHB violated this repeatedly and worse, selectively, looking only at random pieces presented only by Mrs. Carson. The question before the Board was **not** how many drafts there were. The drafts were not before the AHB for action. Even if the AHB thought they were, having admitted two hours would not be long enough, they did not act correctly on the issue, refusing to look at all drafts or the same parts in all drafts or any parts not presented falsely and maliciously by Mrs. Carson. The matter was not considered by paragraph or as a whole.

Obviously, the AHB did not adopt *Robert's Rules of Order* as their parliamentary authority. One wonders then if they had any authority. Were they technically a deliberative assembly or just a platform for the extension of prejudice? The question was never considered informally, by agreement anyway.

Obviously, the procedure is different because the AHB is a small board (in every sense of the word), as it is for this group, of less than a dozen members. The rules, therefore, are slightly different from those of large groups. For instance, members are not required to obtain the floor before speaking, which they can do while seated. No limit to number of times a member can speak to a question. The chair can speak without rising. But other rules of order do apply. All of them.

I notice that the thesis committee counted the number of interruptions. I

# The Thesis

was so curious that I counted them also. The 114 interruptions they counted was just the number of times the transcribing typist said interruptions. The actual number was far higher, I'm sure, over 210 interruptions, of which 73 were mine; I think 100% of mine were justified. Numbers are fascinating aren't they? I have some more statistics. Regarding long quotes, Mr. Romeo had 4 quotes over 55 lines each with only 10 lines of commentary. Mr. Rhodes, for example had 4 quotes totaling 37 lines with only 11 lines of commentary within 1.5 pages.

Oh, here's an interesting set. Mrs. Carson always wanted the thesis shorter than it was. When it was 250 pages, she wanted 150, when 186—that's the 7th draft, the approved one, remember,—she urged 120. When it was 160 pages, she suggested 100. And when it was 120 pages she demanded that it be 60. She was almost consistent in wanting it smaller, but she had no idea how small.

Carson: Wrong! I did. Most theses are well under 100 pages.

Moon: (Leigh I Carson, are you a 'garlic in shoe?' 'or chasing lie?')

Cant: Avoided censure again, did you? I wonder where you got that figure. There are over 218 theses in the library over 200 pages; over 500—I lost track of the exact count—over 100 pages. Maybe 300 under 100 pages. The mean number of pages would appear to be well over 150 pages.

Moving on to specific errors, please look at appendix B. Each documented example is composed of three parts: my text from the 7th draft, one of my professors erroneous corrections, and a quote from a recognized authority on the subject. In the first series, page 1, line 2, I stated "Plato was the first ... to ask about art as an imitation of life." Mr. Finn wrote: "Plato—No!" I quote from Eva Schaper, in *Prelude to Aesthetics*, page 42: "This sense of imitation is dominant in the 'Ion' and it is retained throughout the 'Republic' ..." On page 1, line 13, I state "artifacts ... are structured like living organisms." Mr. Finn has penciled in "Not Plato or Aristotle!" On page 89 of—

Duran: Mr. Cant, I'm sorry but your time is almost up. You should start your summary.

Cant: Well, fortunately, it's all written down in the 80 pages of the five appendices supplied to each of you. I trust you have gone through them. It's quite revealing. For instance, Mrs. Carson fares no better, but then she attacked more than 3 pages. For instance, I wrote "In ... intentional being we are a subject opposed to an object" on page 5. Mrs. Carson crossed it out and wrote "in relation to, not opposed." Merleau-Ponty had written on page 213 of *The Visible and the Invisible*, "I describe perception as a diacritical ... oppositional system ..."

Mr. Kraft never wrote anything, so he made no specific errors, just general ones, such as calling it "incoherent." The charge of incoherence seems to be the last refuge of the critically inept. The grammatical corrections were even worse. I'll give just one example of that. On page 8 of the 7th draft, the 12th sentence is a complex sentence. Mrs. Carson mistakenly corrected it as a run-on sentence; it is not.

In summary, my committee gave contradictory directions and made erroneous corrections on a thesis they did not apparently understand or even read carefully. Having no grammatical or philosophical reason to reject it, they rejected it on terms of "style," as Mrs. Carson testified to the—

Carson: Where!

Cant: Page 51 of the transcript—to the AHB. This is not a proper or sufficient reason. The AHB was wrong to accept it as such. There findings should be overturned for this and many other demonstrated reasons.

Duran: Now, does anyone of the respondents have a response?

Finn: Yes, you do not deserve the degree. You are temperamental and ingrateful. You were wrong to bring your problems to either hearing board. Your work is incoherent! The AHB couldn't decide because they were in different fields, but we—

Cant: How dare you tell me that the committee could not decide if the thesis was incoherent or ungrammatical because they were in different disciplines like home ec or ag econ! All of you should have the same basic skills with communication or you should not be teaching! You should be teaching your students how to speak and write well, not how to get a job as an electronic technical writer or television broadcaster or agricultural grant writer. If they can't speak or write, knowing what a diode is or seed pod is won't help.

Carson: You cannot get away with this false honesty. You will not get the degree from an appeal committee. We would have helped you. Why did you do this? Is it worth it? You surely will fail.

Moon: (He could only fail, Carson, by your criteria of 'cash religion' or being 'gasoline rich.')

Cant: I've failed before. It's just a limitation of my self. If I fail, I will fail. I will admit it and go on. You have failed me, but I have failed you. The only solution is for all of us to be judged by our betters and go on from there. But, you the university have real boundaries, too. Learning and reciting facts only does so much. The culture that surrounds and the nature that surrounds or perhaps intertwines throughout cannot be reached by books or facts. Humility and reverence are needed, discipline and flexibility also, to succeed.

You have said that you will fail if I get this degree by tricking you. You've already failed, by graduating students who think it okay to misspell the titles in their thesis, who plagiarize their research from published books, and who do not care if they behave honestly to others. But you don't care, because you are like them! You do not know how to speak or write. You don't even know that you don't know, because you reinforce each other. You are not honest—not to your colleagues or to your spouses, and not to yourselves! You are not even responsible adults, just inept paper prostitutes! Should I have to learn the value of a good education by getting a poor one? Should I be prepared for good teachers only by

## The Thesis

being mistreated by bad ones?

Moon: (Poor, Walter, just a 'bleak winter cat' of 'wet Cant caliber')

Duran: Mr. Cant . . . I don't know what to say to you. The committee may now ask questions of the respondents. Are there any questions?

Cohn: Yes, I, uhm, Professor Carson, did you think that, in your sentence that Mr. Cant, ah, claims is proof of your acceptance, did you, ah, mean it to be an absolute acceptance or a qualification?

Moon: (Cohn, Larson J., an odd-looking man apparently still in the process of integrating his body parts into one being; nothing fit: the lips were wrong, the nose too small, the hands tiny, the belly large—even the clothes seemed mismatched. Larson Cohn: Just one of the 'acne lords' who 'scorn deal' with the 'snarl coed' because he's a 'saner clod;' say what you will, the 'clod nears' cleverness.)

Carson: Yes, I did qualify it. Look. I said "I think" and then later I said "after." That was certainly not an absolute approval.

Cohn: And did you precede, er, follow this reluctant conditional approval with specific objections and lacuna?

Moon: (There's that word lacuna again, misused, or maybe used properly if Professor Carson's was the missing part. Cohn: one of the 'crone lads,' a bright 'censor lad' who can 'clean rods' in the 'solder can' without hurting his 'olden scar.' I wonder if he is Jewish, like Wittgenstein. Wittgenstein, who admitted late in life that he was 75% Jewish, took pains to conceal his Jewish heritage. With Wittgenstein, privacy lead to mystery, and obscurity—of personality and thought—to greatness of influence. What was not written was the more important part of his philosophy to him. Ethics, I think. With Cohn, the privacy conceals only emptiness. Cohn and Duran must have read only the written part of Wittgenstein and not understood the missing ethics.)

Carson: Yes, thank you for emphasizing that. There were three pages of specific objections as well as the general objections on content and style.

Ekerd: Professor Carson, did you think Cant ignored or defied your warnings that he must correct the lacuna of lucidity and coherence in his thesis?

Carson: Yes, repeatedly. He never made it clear what he was doing.

Ekerd: Professor Finn, was Mr. Cant intractable with regard to your corrections?

Moon: (D. Wally Ekerd: the 'lewd lard key' or 'lewd dry leak' who 'just raked lewdly?' She seemed to be concerned with nailing the coffin shut on Cant's dead aspirations to be a philosopher)

Finn: He certainly was. He went beyond that, beyond intractability, with his spurious errors and constant name-changes—he enjoyed it. He was pleased when he fooled us. I am paid to teach philosophy. Therefore, I must know something about it. He has not respected that.

Duran: Are there any more questions? If not—

Cant: Yes, do you intend to read any of the proofs I offer you—anything to break the deadlock of my word against theirs?

Moon: (Poor Walter, can the 'attacker blew-in' 'win cake battle' with just a 'nickel water bat?' or is he just a 'wet bank article?')

Duran: That is not our function. If there are no questions, this hearing is closed.

Moon: (I was almost overcome by the smelly gangrene of professors. Maybe Marinetti was right that we needed to be freed from them, as we needed to be free from the many museums and institutions that rest on us like gravestones compressing our living hearts.)

Hill on Golf Course Run

## 25 Power

"They have the power over me, so I will have to do something they say, or just give up." I concluded this, sitting in her office.

"Power is a funny thing. Who does get power and how? Tribal leaders had authority but not a lot of power; if you disagreed, you could walk away and start your own tribe. Tribal authority came from knowing more and acting more effectively, say, in the hunt. Leaders were chosen for their knowledge, then given power through ritual means. Authority is associated with power to command."

"And, if you choose not to obey the command?"

"Chiefs in larger communities had some power, to give away surplus or enforce taboos. Kings, on the other hand, got power from keeping the surplus food. Kings claimed to get power from a god; the surplus food was the proof. After a while, they get power from a monopoly on weapons and violence. Religious leaders often get power from a god or from people's belief. Feudal or corporate lords get power from wealth and from the disparities in income."

"I can feel the disparities. Where did Bono get his power to decide my fate?"

"I daresay from the university, which is allowed certain powers by society. In nontribal societies, like ours here, the ritual and the vestment of power is passed to someone without true authority. Power can be linked to exploitation when it is used to benefit a small elite and to advance their interests. Power can be pursued just for the sake of power. Institutions and power structures are assembled from rules of behavior that allow decision-making."

"Yes, without authority or knowledge apparently. But all power is not the same. Kings coerce their subjects into submission by threatening sanctions. Chiefs compensate for their use of power by offering rewards."

"Yea, and Presidents and Ministers get power from being elected, often as a result of manipulation of facts or votes within the system. The exercise of power is inevitable in society, whether it is a band of fifty people or an empire of millions. Maybe power increases with conflicts of interest."

"Communities can be more effective if someone can make decisions when there are conflicts of interest."

"The Prez?"

"Maybe. Relations of cultural power are defined culturally by agreements on positions of authority that emerge from rules of conduct. If I were you I would follow most of the rules and just protest the one deviant problem, the thesis."

" I can see how small communities with fast decisions would have an advantage with anarchistic communities, but an academic community?"

"Doesn't apply. It's shielded from stupidity by all the surplus."

"Maybe I should just leave."

## 26  Proposing New Faculty Honors

May 10, 1976

Dear Spudnut Editor:

We have become increasingly concerned about finding a suitable way to honor our wise and altruistic faculty and administration. Therefore, we would like to propose that these academic ~~gnats~~ giants each have a unique dessert named in their honor at the Student Union. What could be more appropriate to celebrate their contributions to this magnificent university and to do justice to their incomparable stature as persons in integrity and ~~accidental~~ educational excellence. Here are our suggestions for a menu of fountain fantasies:

- The Hunter Humdinger—gobs and gobs of whipped cream piled on mounds of more whipped cream. Extra whipped cream. $1
- The Cordoner Commemoration—a bouffant of peppermint ice cream and fudge, laced with ~~arsenic~~ anise. Extra whipped cream. $2
- The Cohn slimmer—1 scoop of vanilla with cottage cheese and pickle. $1 (may require $20 surcharge)
- The Regents Dinner—a smorgasbord of flavors (vanilla only) covered with a rainbow of syrups (vanilla only). You must be vanilla to order it. $1
- The Aerodrome Gift—A quarter scoop of pistachio in a three-pint dish. You pay a small percentage ($2.50) of the development costs, the remainder is subsidized, but only Kibblesford gets to eat it.
- Strand's Last Grant—an empty dish garnished with a cherry and peanuts. $585 (but funding is available)
- The Committee Coherence—Flounder and chili covered with marshmallows, mayonnaise, and yoghurt, with a scoop of raisin ice cream, served directly on the counter top—you'll need your fingers for this one! And it only costs $0.10 or $1 or $7.83 or ...
- Ralph's Retribution—You pick a flavor but he only approves what he wants you to have; no substitutions, drops, or adds. You've already paid for it.
- Gorton's Grabber—A scoop of prune-lemon sherbet on a lake of collard juice, spiced with tabasco sauce. Eating is payment enough.
- Pilgrim's Promise—The service person takes your order and your money. Call back in a week to see if you can get it.
- The ASIMU Candidate—2 scoops of each flavor ice cream with 2 dollops of each topping, served in a wheelbarrow. Donations of $15

accepted.
- The Hearing Board Fiddle-Fodder—Someone in the Student Union picks a flavor for you; you are forced to eat it. Someone in Administration chooses a price that you are forced to pay. You asked for it!
- The PE Fandango—French fries in beer covered with chocolate and pineapple—all you can stomach. Paid for by the university with proof of athletic scholarship.
- Grackle's Gasp—You apply for a scoop of strawberry. If you are female, you get it, but if you are male, you leave. Paid for by government agencies interested in transtemporal equality in everything for everyone.
- The Carson Cutback—Three scoops of grape ice over sliced apples. No longer offered to save on costs, you can read about it and it would have cost only $0.25.

What are we waiting for?
~~Walter Cant~~ Wilfred of Idle ho'

## 27 Running at Night

I was only half a mile from the apartment and riding like the wind, so to speak, when I heard the lights and siren behind me. Damn, caught again! I pulled over and stood by the bike. It was almost pitch black except for a distant streetlight.

Officer Dunlevy came up and said, "Walter, for the fourth time, you have to get a light for that!"

"Oh, come on, officer, sir, you know my argument, if everyone else has a light, I can see them and take evasive action."

"And you know my reply, if one other person goes without a light and you two meet, I have to clean up the mess."

"Good point, I concede."

"And, it's against the law. So next time I catch you, I will ticket you."

"That is fair, and I will not argue."

"Arguing is fine. My shift can be boring. But, get the damn light, or next time …"

I put down the bike and went over and leaned on the hood next to him, "Does Chief Hudson know you're cutting me slack again?"

"What do you want to argue about?"

"Gas prices, I think. Should they be higher or lower?"

"What? Lower. Any idiot can see that."

"I think they should be higher, at least taxed higher."

"Why?" Dunlevy asked incredulously.

"To pay for all the subsidized things that are necessary. Not just roads and bridges, but health-related problems."

"That's just wrong. Higher taxes would depress the economy that needs to be healthy to provide those services—"

While the discussion was progressing I was thinking about taking another route tomorrow night or maybe running. I wondered if he would anticipate that?

I have been sending out applications for schools. That is hard, having already attended seven schools with no success at a degree. Each year I seem to add a new area of concentration. Each year I seem to master some aspects of it, often enough to get a job in that field without a degree. And, now I am looking again. Fortunately, I have been doing well in Botany, despite the number of classes I had to change to audits. I have coauthored a few papers—in fact, one of them is being used at the Cow College next door to demonstrate how to write a thesis using the Script computer program—now there is an irony.

The application to Georgia was finished and sent. Sometimes I wonder if it would be possible to combine every interest in one article or book. Would I be a metaphysicotheologicocosmologist, then, like Voltaire said?

## 28 Form without Substance? Losing Round 5

May 19, 1976

Report Of Faculty Council Ad Hoc Committee For Walter Cant Appeal
Members of Committee: Glasgot Duran (Chm.), Larson J. Cohn, D. Wally Ekerd.

This Appeal Committee was appointed by the Faculty Council to act for it in hearing an appeal by Mr. Walter Cant from the decision of the Academic Hearing Board regarding his master's degree thesis.

The Academic Hearing Board had affirmed the decision of Mr. Cant's thesis committee not to approve his thesis. On March 22, 1976, this Appeal Committee distributed to participants in the appeal a copy of rules adopted by the Committee for the conduct of the appeal. A copy of those rules is attached hereto as an appendix. Each side in the appeal filed written arguments in accordance with those rules. The Committee reviewed the file of the Academic Hearing Board in this matter and a transcript of the hearing conducted by the Academic Hearing Board on May 15, 1975. The Committee held its own hearing on May 5, 1976. Present at the hearing were Mr. Cant, the members of his thesis committee (Professors Kraft, Carson and Finn), and Dean Karen G. Hard of the Graduate School, who attended as an observer.

Mr. Cant alleges that four errors were committed by the Academic Hearing Board: "they did not use *Robert's Rules of Order*, or any rules of order, as stipulated in the University Handbook; they accepted irrelevant mouthings from Professor Carson, Finn and Kraft; they ignored the admissions of errors by Carson, Kraft and Finn, and they overlooked the conclusive written evidence that I had followed the ambiguous directions of Mrs. Carson; finally, they even drew the wrong conclusions from the testimony they did accept." (From Mr. Cant's March 26, 1975, petition to the Appeal Committee.)

The first two alleged errors are procedural in nature, while the last two go more to the substantive issues before the Hearing Board. The alleged procedural errors will be discussed first.

Faculty Constitution Article VI provides that *Robert's Rules of Order* shall govern all meetings of faculty committees "in all cases where they are applicable and in which they are not in conflict with . . . rules subsequently adopted by majority vote of . . . faculty committees for the conduct of their respective meetings." *Robert's Rules* are designed for use by deliberative bodies; the rules govern such matters as the making and seconding of motions, the debate of motions, amendment of motions, and referral to committee. *Robert's Rules* can have little application to an evidentiary hearing such as that conducted by the

Academic Hearing Board. At the commencement of the hearing the chairman stated the procedure that would be used and this was, at the very least, acquiesced in by the rest of the board. The procedure was not followed rigidly, but there were no deviations or defects that were prejudicial to the presentation by Mr. Cant of his case.

It is true that there was some irrelevant evidence presented to the Board — by both sides, for that matter. This had the unfortunate effect of wasting time, but it must be remembered that Mr. Cant had ample opportunity to explain to the Board why particular items of evidence were irrelevant and should be disregarded. Mr. Sooner, a member of the Board, pointed this out at one time during the hearing (Transcript p. 12). This is an adequate means of dealing with problems of irrelevant material in a hearing which does not, should not, and cannot pretend to operate with the full rigor of a courtroom trial. There is no basis for concluding that the Academic Hearing Board was prejudiced in reaching its conclusions about the matter in issue by any irrelevant comments that surfaced during the hearing.

This brings us to the substantive issues before the Hearing Board. The Board reached four conclusions:

1. "That Cant has not fulfilled his thesis requirement."
2. "The thesis committee, and particularly Carson, constructively and conscientiously exercised their functions of advising and aiding Cant's work. Indeed, the members of the committee showed commendable forbearance in view of Cant's uncooperative and obstructionist attitude and conduct."
3. "From the beginning of the drafting process and consistently thereafter, the committee made known to Cant the minimum standards necessary for approval of the thesis. The decision to use his own standards and to ignore the admonitions of the committee was Cant's alone. Responsibility for this decision and its consequences remains entirely with Cant."
4. "Cant's thesis has not been definitively rejected. Rather he has been told by all three members of the committee that they have been and are willing to sign a thesis in acceptable form."

The 4th conclusion seems to be a gratuity. Even the 2nd and 3rd are not essential to the Academic Hearing Board's disposition of the case. Suppose (and this is stated only hypothetically rather than in affirmance or rejection of the Board's conclusions) that the thesis committee had been guilty of faulty supervision of the thesis or inappropriate encouragement as to progress. It should be obvious that faulty supervision or inappropriate encouragement could not excuse an unsatisfactory thesis if the degree based on that thesis is to have meaning in terms of respected academic or research standards. Thus, the real issue has to be been whether better the supervise thesis was satisfactory, not whether there could have better supervision.

## The Thesis

Actually the Academic Hearing Board went further than necessary in its first conclusion. It was not up to the Board to find the thesis satisfactory. All the Board had to do was to determine whether the thesis committee acted arbitrarily or discriminatorily in failing to find the thesis satisfactory. We take the Board's first conclusion to reduce to this less strong position, i.e., that it was not established that the thesis committee acted arbitrarily or discriminatorily in rejecting Mr. Cant's thesis. To reach such a conclusion, the Board would have had to determine (a) whether the thesis in fact met the thesis committee's standards and (b) if not, whether the standards themselves were arbitrary or discriminatory.

Regarding these matters, the Academic Hearing Board proceeding is not a model of perfection. But that is not the question. The questions are whether the Board could reasonably have been expected to have examined other evidence than it did and whether its determinations are supported by the evidence before it. Even if the Board did not read Mr. Cant's final product, it would have been of little value for a board made up of history, law, agricultural economics, and home economics professors to read a master's degree thesis in philosophy. Even if the Board did not examine certain intermediate drafts and notes thereon, the crux of the matter was the quality of the final product and the standards for judging that.

While there was conflicting evidence in the case regarding the issues defined in the preceding paragraph, this Appeal Committee cannot say the Board's conclusion (that the thesis committee did not act arbitrarily or discriminatorily in rejecting the thesis) was unsupported by credible evidence.

This Appeal Committee realizes that Mr. Cant still may not have had the kind of inquiry he desires. That kind of review cannot come from an internal University committee. It can come only from a neutral person or committee of persons trained and working in the field of philosophy (and we note that Mr. Cant asked for this at the oral hearing on appeal) or, perhaps, in a court of law. This Appeal Committee makes this observation without any recommendation regarding 'these courses of action. The question of an outside review gets into budgetary considerations that are beyond the province of this Committee. The matter of litigation will have to be a personal decision by Mr. Cant. This Committee wishes to make it clear that the Committee expresses no opinion that there would be any particular prospect of success in litigation nor are we recommending that such action be taken.

In conclusion, this Appeal Committee finds no basis for setting aside the final disposition of the case by the Academic Hearing Board.

## 29 Declaring Eternal Love

"I love you I love you I love you I love you! What movie was that famous quote from?"

"First of all, it wasn't an exact quote. You needed to have at least six more 'I love you's but the movie was 'Singing in the Rain.' Ha!" she answered.

"Well, it wasn't a quote of course, I was just expressing my emotion for you. I was thinking of the first night. It was wonderful, the most wonderful night of my life. We kissed so sweetly, so tenderly, it was like melting seafoam; there was no tension or friction or awkwardness, just an ecstatic union that ... made me speechless."

"And, I was thinking of it, too. That what was missing and what was needed were one—a reliance on something other than myself, an ultimate direction in which to aim myself; a goal for which to reach; this I must! A future good and bright and true of dedication to some overwhelming trust, a thing in which to be reborn, to renew the confidence that whatever I am was not in vain or vanity or a selfish inward thrust that sickens in the end, that rots with sin that corrupts from within. That leaves one, in the end, alone and hollow."

"And, we—"

"No, wait. What wildness and delight! I must let things settle before I can look or understand. Maybe it is just physical. I cannot get too close now. I have my goals in sight. But, I cannot help notice that you were so handsome and strong and gentle."

"Here. I wrote some poetry for you. I'll speak it while you read it:
'I saw you under moonlight and you reflected Me. I saw you under starlight and you grew Distant and mysterious'—" and then I stopped, mesmerized by the expression on her face. I held her so she could not read anymore.

Later, she said, "My experience, my past did not prepare me for this: To love so deeply, so genuinely savor each kiss, and with each embrace lose a measure of will until there is no trace of composure; and rapture not reason burns in my face. Every day I ride crest after crest. And the days in succession build to some towering wave that will either lift us beyond the wall or destroy us on the ground."

I held her, finally speechless at last, and trusted the silence would be enough.

## 30 Epistle to the Jewel of the Gem State University

19 May 1976

Dear President Garnet:
I heartily appeal the Decision of the Faculty Council Ad Hoc In Partem Committee on my case. I direct you to have prepared a transcript of that meeting and to consider this new appeal.

The Committee followed its procedures fairly and rigorously. However, the Committee did **not** perform its avowed function to review the actions of the Academic Hearing Board (AHB). The Committee intended to "review the transcript in the case and consider argument on the questions of whether the Academic Hearing Board followed proper procedures, whether it inquired into the appropriate issues, and whether its findings and conclusions are supported by the evidence at the hearing." (memo, 22 March 1976) what the Committee did do must be treated in more detail. in general the Committee simply approved the AHB's improper procedures; it found that only one issue—"whether the thesis was satisfactory" (Report, p.4) was appropriate, and that the AHB considered this, among other inappropriate issues; and, after admitting that "It was not up to the Board to find the thesis satisfactory" (Report, p.4), the Committee decided that the AHB's conclusion that the thesis was not satisfactory was supported by the evidence at the hearing, although the Committee refused to look at that evidence.

Specific samples of the Report of the Faculty Council Committee are even more disturbing.

> (1) The Committee claims that Robert's Rules of Order were not applicable to the AHB, and that rules adopted by majority vote could be substituted, according to the Faculty Constitution. The Committee then admits that the AHB did <u>not</u> adopt Mr. Dodd's rules by majority vote. The Committee admits furthermore that the informal procedure "was not followed rigidly" (Report, p. 2) yet contends that the deviations were not prejudicial to my case.
> 
> (2) The Committee admits that there was "irrelevant evidence presented" (Report, p.2), but contends that it did not prejudice the conclusions of the AHB. It claims that my explanation was "an adequate means of dealing with Problems of irrelevant material' (Report, p.3)
> 
> (3) In considering the four conclusions of the AHB on the substantive issues, the Committee discards the 4th conclusion as "a gratuity." (Report, p.3) Then the Committee states that the 2nd and 3rd "are not essential to the

Academic Hearing Board's disposition of the case." (Report, p.3) Thus they conclude that faulty supervision and inappropriate encouragement are not real issues. Finally the Committee treats the first conclusion of the AHB: 'Actually the Academic Hearing Board went further than necessary in its first conclusion. It was not up to the Board to find the thesis satisfactory." (Report, p.4) Only after completely rewriting the findings of the AHB can the Faculty Committee conclude that it "finds no basis for setting aside the final disposition of the case" (Report, p.6)

(4) The Committee admits that the AHB proceeding "is not a model of perfection." (Report, p.4) This point is then dismissed as not being the question. The Committee cites the question as being whether the AHB could have examined other evidence and whether its determinations were supported by the evidence it did consider. Then the Committee concedes that the AHB did examine some of the thesis (part of a 4th draft, falsely presented by Dr. Carson as the last draft, AHB Transcript, p.25) and that "there was conflicting evidence in the case..." (Report, p.5) In spite of that, the committee double-negatively concludes: "this Appeal Committee cannot say the Board's conclusion... was unsupported by credible evidence." (Report, p.5 )

(5) Although the Committee offers pregnant hints about external review for the thesis, about litigation, and about budgetary considerations, it conveniently has no opinions or recommendations. (Report, p.5)

The Faculty Committee was unable to disprove any of the four errors of the AHB. Indeed, the meanders of the Committee admitted that the AHB did not follow Robert's Rules of Order, and that the AHB did not even follow their own informal procedure. (Report, p.2) Secondly, the Committee admitted that there was "irrelevant evidence presented" (Report, p. 2) Thirdly the committee allowed there was "conflicting evidence" (Report, p. 5) in the drafts, and admitted that the final product, which was judged by the AHB, was not even examined. And finally, the Committee acknowledged that the AHB drew the wrong conclusions. (Report, p. 4) In fact the Committee had to <u>rewrite</u> the decision of the AHB to match their own biased and unsupported conclusions. The written evidence I submitted has yet to be examined. The Report of the Faculty Committee was a senseless exercise in. evasion and a pointless illustration of the elasticity of logic.

Although the Faculty Committee hinted at them, the real problems have not been considered. They are outlined here:

(A) My major professor, Mrs. Carson, misled me through drafts and styles. There is written evidence of this. The two other members of the Master's Committee, Mr. Kraft and Mr. Finn, were indifferent to six of the drafts and refused to read them. There is written evidence of this.

(B). When these professors did evaluate the 7th draft, they did so

erroneously, displaying incredible ignorance of English grammar and their own subject matters (Art and Philosophy). There is written evidence for this.
(C) When I informed Dean Strand of this, he agreed to have my thesis sent out for external review. Two months later Dean Strand found arbitrary reasons for not doing so. After initially agreeing to send it out, President Garnet has supported Dean Strand's reversal.
(D) After requesting and receiving official mediation on my thesis, my Master's Committee violated faculty ethics to subject me to defamation. There is incredible written evidence of this.
(E) Although the university and the Master's Committee have been unable to define any standards for a thesis, my thesis is unequivocally worthy of a degree here. There is undeniable evidence of this. My thesis has been compared to those of Mrs. Carson's last two students, Romeo and Rhodes, quite favorably; it has received good reviews from other professors and publishers; and parts of it have been published.

I have appealed these matters, specifically, before the AHB and the Faculty Council, not to mention Dean Strand, President Garnet, and the Regents (Letters: 20 October 1975, 3 November 1975, 16 December 1975, 31 January 1976, 9 April 1976, et. al.) Everyone concerned has chosen to ignore them, for whatever reasons, fear or irresponsibility. Eventually, the faculty and administration will have to consider these matters, through litigation, appeals, more appeals, or sheer embarrassment. I ask that you short-circuit the inevitable calamity, by overruling the Report of the Faculty Council Committee, and by bringing this shameful episode to a proper conclusion; either send the thesis out, or have some committee examine **all** of the evidence, or simply have Duran hand me the degree that I have already earned several times over.

Sincerely,
Walter B. Cant

## *31 Preparing for Exile*

I was afraid to have her see me packing, so I came back to the apartment and sorted my things. Triage of the material things: Those I could do without, those I might need later, and those that were critical to have now. And, what was in the last category? My manuscripts and articles, my favorite clothes and shoes, a few athletic medals, my grandfather's pocket watch, and some letters and photos.

I put them in boxes and took them downstairs. I cleaned up the apartment a little and did the dishes from our breakfast or tea and toast with raspberry jam. Then I took the bike back to work in the library.

On the Way

## 32 Another Facet, Another Reflection

June 1, 1976

Another meeting with the President. Walter at least likes to go to the top, even if it's just for comforting words. Walter was wearing a tie with a beautiful design—the moon and stars against a midnight blue background—badly tied, however, so I showed him how to do a Windsor knot. He has nice hands. We left from the library together at 2:00. The President and Graduate Dean were already sitting in Garnet's office talking about something. The new industrial, grey-green, all-weather carpet was recent. The paneling was in the process of being removed; the plaster underneath was water-stained.

Garnet: —and that's what the vote should be like. Oh, they're here. Walter, Ellsin. Could you please wait in the outer office. We'll be through in a minute. Thank you.

Moon: (So we waited. The secretary was doing little things like moving papers and adjusting the phones on her desk, looking good while she did—for the life of me I could not figure out what she was doing. Walter was sighing heavily, torturing his papers. The Prez opened the door and nodded to his last visitors, before addressing us.)
Garnet: Thank you for waiting. Have a seat. Coffee?
Moon: Coffee for me please. (Garnet was wearing a fantastic red cotton blouse with raised designs—ah, for the salary of a president.)
Cant: Nothing, thank you. I just had some water.
Strand: Fasting for the resistance?
Cant (smiling): No, really, I never learned to like tea or coffee. I was disturbed by the letter I just got from Vice President Bono, telling me that all channels open to me in my appeal are exhausted and the matter is closed. What did he mean?
Garnet: Walter, what is your ambition? No, no, I mean, do you intend to teach, do research, write? Not everyone likes to jump into a debate as soon as they meet.
Cant: Research, I guess, in ecology. I'm leaving tomorrow for Athens. I'm going to summer school at the University of Georgia. I might get a fellowship.
Strand: Why don't you just do what your committee wants and finish first?
Cant: I tried that two years ago. They still don't know what they want. Besides, do you believe that any of them would give me a recommendation now? It was hard enough in ecology here, since my faculty know their faculty and go to parties together.

Garnet: I sympathize with you. You know who had a career like yours? Professor Finn. He started out in chemistry, then went into physical engineering, and finished in philosophy. I can't understand why you two don't hit it off.

Cant: Yes, I know. He told me once when he was helping me move into Leigh's basement. Different style maybe. I don't make instant decisions like he does—or did 30 years ago and then just repeats.

Garnet (sighing): Vice President Bono meant that you have no more avenues of appeal through the university, no more hearing boards or ad hoc committees. I confess. There seems to be such a wide variance in perception among the principals involved: You, the committee, the graduate school, and the committees. I find myself unable to assess clearly what are the sources of distress and how to track them to the current impasse. I think—

Cant: I can outline them very simply.

Moon: (I was doodling, again. About Garnet's name. I suppose I do this because there might be a hidden meaning in the name, like a hidden meaning in the sum of numbers of a birthday or arrangement of the stars, but mostly because it's fun. I feel better about people when I play with their names. It's an advantage, as if they had to appear naked at a meeting in which only I was dressed.)

Garnet: Please. Let me finish. I think there are a few things that can be nailed down, and these things can lead to a solution, if you follow through on them. First, your dropping your enrollment in philosophy and enrolling in ecology while the matter of your thesis in philosophy was pending was not helpful. If you are sincere in your desire to pursue a final judgment in—on your thesis as part of your qualification for a degree in philosophy, then I believe you must re-enroll in philosophy.

Moon: (Garnet's name could be: "he stranger nut." Or "strange hunter.")

Cant: But, I've been a biology student for over a year!

Strand: This would be temporary, until the thesis is decided. Anticipating your next interruption, it would not effect your credits in ecology, since you cannot graduate with a Ph.D. for another year, at the very least, I suspect. Furthermore, I will even do the necessary paperwork for you or reregister you in philosophy, if this is still your desire. I have gone over the regulations with Hunter, and we are in firm agreement on this point. Without your reregistration, it is futile for you to pursue the thesis, since we cannot award the degree to a nonregistrant.

Cant: Your position has a certain charming logical contradiction. Please remember that I was enrolled in philosophy when I finished my requirements, and that—

Strand: You are not finished. You will not be fin—

Garnet: It's okay, Karl. Let him finish—hmmm.

Moon: (Karl says 'gunners hatter' surely an important function in the navy, an 'entrant gusher,' to 'hearten grunts.' He would 'shun garter net,' to 'gather sun rent.' Maybe it didn't mean anything anymore.)

Cant: —that Professor Carson authorized my taking 20 credit hours of courses in biology last January. I should not need to be enrolled in philosophy just because I am appealing a decision made while I was enrolled. Furthermore, if I change majors now, it will alienate even more of my biology professors who have serious doubts that I am serious as it is. After all, I write letters to you and the President and various committees once a week.

Garnet: Walter, I really sympathize with you. I am spending a lot of my time following this drama in which you have chosen to involve me. If you would just reregister, or let Dean Strand do it, then the thesis could be completed and submitted in final form to the Dean, who will also see to it that the members of your committee. read it and evaluate it. Then, if the—

Cant: Please, forgive me for interrupting. I understand that you may not keep perfectly current on the tiresome soap opera—what shall we call it, the "The Young and Degreeless"?—but I finished the thesis over a year ago. It has been ready to be read and approved, but no one will read it!

Garnet: Humor me, please. Just tell everyone you rewrote it. Give it to the Dean with a new abstract or something. He will shepherd it through. And, if it is positive, if they give an affirmative recommendation to the Dean, then the matter is settled, the oral can be arranged and you can finished. If you pass, the degree can be awarded. If negative, if the philosophy department cannot accept it, we will send it off-campus to referees selected by him from suggestions made by you and the members of your committee. If they like it, if their evaluation contradicts the your committee's, we are willing to accept it and arrange for a final oral examination.

Strand: And, if the outside referees concur with the in-house committee, that your work is not considered to be an acceptable thesis document, we shall consider the matter settled in this wise. Then, it would be incumbent on you to accept the fact that you either cannot write or at least have not written an acceptable thesis and drop the matter there. You would then be free to pursue the matter of reregistration in botany if, as it now seems, this is your ultimate goal.

Cant: My ultimate goal is death. But—

Strand: All right, penultimate goal, then.

Cant: My penultimate goal is reshaping the world. Perhaps, we can settle on the idea of 'next' goal, which it certainly is. I am willing to accept such a judgment. I have been begging, crying, challenging for the opportunity. I think, however, it goes without saying that, if the review is positive, it is incumbent on my professors to admit that they cannot write or judge writings in philosophy. Will you make sure they are free to pursue another profession, such as sanitary engineering?

Strand: What do you mean?

Cant: Give me their jobs. They can have mine. I will teach philosophy in a disciplined and circumspect way, showing more flexibility and understanding than they have.

Garnet (smiling): I'm afraid their sins, if they are such, would not be that serious. They may have made a bad judgment, but they are not incompetent.

Cant: I spent several days documenting their errors and lack of competence in philosophy. I have the errors in their own handwriting and I have Xeroxed pages of the corrections.

Strand: Making errors does not make one incompetent.

Moon: (I fidgeted. Karl O. Strand: 'or drank salt,' 'or Kant's lard,' or 'rod rank salt.' My doodling was becoming meaningless.

Cant: Does refusing to admit the errors?

Strand: No, not that either.

Cant: President Garnet, would you look at the errors?

Garnet: No, I cannot. I do not have the time, even if it was my function in the university. You have had a chance to introduce the errors into hearings.

Cant: They were ignored. No one ever looked at them.

Garnet: I am the President of all the university. I cannot decide in favor of one above another, regardless of the justification.

Cant: I found many more errors by many more students and faculty. As you know I work in the library. I read as much as I can as it comes through the cataloging area. Theses are a favorite of mine, now. I have Xeroxed copies of 14—14!—theses or dissertations at the university within the past two years that have misspellings in the title or abstract. In the title, for God's sake!

Strand: 14? How many with misspellings in the title?

Cant: 6. How did these ever get through the normal process of appeal?

Garnet: I'm amazed. If it's true, it doesn't reflect very well on scholarship at this university, does it?

Moon: Perhaps it's time to implement an alumni reevaluation program—issue the academic recalls.

Garnet: Not amusing.

Cant: No, and it gets worse. In the last appeal, to the ad hoc faculty committee, I compared specifically parts of my thesis with those by Romeo and Rhodes, recent graduates of the department. I showed that everything I was criticized for, such as long quotes and long paragraphs, they were guilty of doing to excess. Dr. Carson and the ad hocers thought that was irrelevant. When I looked more closely at Mr. Rhodes's thesis, I found examples of plagiarism—

Strand: What? Be careful here!

Cant: For example, I have a page from Kockelmans' book on Heidegger. Here on page 75 is a statement by Kockelmans that appears unacknowledged, word for word, on page 23 of Rhodes's thesis. There's another one on—

Strand: Walter, Eric already was awarded his thesis. That is not the issue here.

Cant: Exactly my point. He was rewarded with a degree for sloppy punctuation, long paragraphs and uncited borrowings. By the same people refusing me—

Strand: Are you certain that there are none of those in yours?

Cant: I am sure, and I'm willing to let anyone read it who will. Really sure. Really willing.

Garnet: What do you intend to do with this information?

Cant: I reported my findings to Finn and Carson. They can do what they will. I suspect they will do nothing. That's the pattern. What will you do? Doesn't this lower the value of any degree from here?

Moon: (Why then is he fighting for a degree from here? If it is worth do little? But, I knew he was right; I have been complaining about misspellings and plagiarism for years—it is worse than he knows.)

Strand: I am aware of it now. The standards can be tightened for future candidates.

Cant: For me?

Strand: If you re-enroll.

Cant: If I were a vindictive person, I would go to the newspaper with these facts. I would do everything in my power to embarrass and humiliate the university and its faculty. I would write to the governor, go on television, mock the graduates at every conference and public forum. Shower examples of mediocrity and idiocy on everyone within hearing or reading. I would tear down the reputation and the worth of the university just to satisfy my anger and rage at being unfairly treated. I would tear down the differences, word by word, degree by degree until only my thesis remained as a marker of what had been a fairly decent land grant school useful for teaching farmers how to kill every living thing but wheat. I'd do it. I'd feel badly, but no more badly than I feel now, at my mistreatment. But, I'm not vindictive. I will only suggest a few measures to help the university avoid pissing on its own shoes. For example, hiring a university editor to read all theses. I have more suggestions here. I'll leave them with you.

Garnet: Perhaps you have been mistreated, but you have the power to correct that. The Dean has recommended that procedure to you, specific procedure to resolve the difficulties you've encountered. Reregister, please.

Cant: I cannot do that. I am a graduate student in a different discipline now.

Moon: Perhaps I might suggest a compromise. What if the thesis was sent out or whatever. If it is approved extramurally, then he could register for the degree and reregister the following semester in ecology.

Strand: Cannot be done that way. Has to be immediate.

Cant: Why? Their position is logically untenable and indefensible. This is a new requirement by Dean Strand. I have been registered in ecology for three semesters and a summer school. Why—

Strand: Not so! I demanded this as soon as I found out that you had changed. Two months ago, I think.

Cant: Maybe, but that's not all. You now ask me to resubmit a retyped draft to a redundant committee. He—you—ask me to send out a draft that was uncorrected of my professors mistakes so they can verify it as the same one they rejected—they rejected them all!—but you have already told me that I can finish a corrected draft, which I have. You are all paralyzed by contradiction.

Garnet: Listen, what if I were to ask Dean Strand to waive any special requirements that might apply to your case for reenrollment in philosophy and then reenrollment in ecology? Karl, what do you think?

Strand: I could eliminate the red tape, if Walter will reregister.

Garnet: Well, Walter? The ball is in your court.

Cant: I could not re-enroll. I'm sorry. I'm usually a very flexible person, willing to compromise and refit, err, you know, fit in, but my committee has pushed me beyond my tolerance limit for agreeing to illogical actions.

Garnet: And, what about the second point here. I do not find anything unreasonable in Dean Strand's holding that the thesis be in final form and be submitted to your thesis committee before going to an off-campus board. Obviously, if—

Cant. President Garnet. I'm sorry. There is nothing unreasonable in this gesture as an isolated case, but I have been asked to do similar things for over two years, with no result and no satisfaction. It may not be unreasonable to whip a dog once to discipline him, but it is dangerous to whip him one more time, the 40th time, and expect obedience. I cannot do either.

Strand: Well, that's that, then.

Cant: I guess I'll have to be resolved to just getting my thesis published as a book. The reviewers seem to be very positive about it, and the publisher thinks it might be marketable, marginally, since the topic is philosophy—

Strand: You sent it out to be rev—

Garnet: Published? You mean—

Moon: Oh, no, you weren't going to bring that up.

Strand: Did you send it out to reviewers?

Cant: Yes, I sent it to three professors at three universities as—please, let me finish—as a book manuscript, not as a disputed rejection. One was not interested. One liked it and recommended it to a student of his at Northwestern, and the other suggested a publisher who might be interested.

Garnet: Who is the publisher?

Cant: Dedham Press in Massachusetts. I brought the letter.

Garnet: All right. It's your trump to play.

Cant: "Dear Mr. Cant, I have just received the report on your work and we would like to publish it. ... Although several editors thought that the sales potential is uncertain, the general feeling is that the book will do well in its niche."

Strand: May I? Thanks. It's on the letterhead. Here: "We can offer you a standard royalty contract. You will want to return the papers as soon"—well, congratulations.

Garnet: Yes, congratulations.

Moon: (Maybe the 'rebel win attack' of Walter Cant has 'beaten law trick' to 'win back a letter.' Perhaps he will 'recant bleak wit' with a 'wet black retina' from the 'bleak titan crew' after all.)

Strand: I'm afraid it won't change the procedure at all, though. You must do those two simple things that we have been urging. I am willing to consider Ellsin's compromise, but I'd prefer immediate legislation, oh registration, I mean reregistration.

Cant: With all due respect, I cannot. I feel like I am locked in a meaningless circle. There is something futile about asking the administration to criticize its faculty's behavior. The futility is justified by my privileged observation of the comic effect of everyone from the lowliest professor to assuming grotesque postures to maintain a fictional dignity while trying to punish the questioner at all costs. The faculty and administration, even you I'm afraid, Mr. President, try so hard to avoid real issues and responsibilities that they have all lost sight of the goals: Education, enlightenment. That reminds me. I read once that, in India, street beggars maimed their own children so that they might survive better as beggars. Is the university reduced to this? Maiming students so that they might survive outside?

Garnet: Walter, you know I am sympathetic. And, sometimes with your rampant portrayals of us, it is hard for me to remain sympathetic. I have heard Karl say that he thought your original treatment by the committee was, well, something he wouldn't have stood for himself. We want you really want you to get the degree, to go on to your next challenge in life, but we are bound by the rules adopted by the university. We cannot set them aside for you.

Cant: Gentlemen, I am grateful for your time and your scholarly demeanor. I will think about your offer, but I cannot promise that I can go through one, or two, more hoops. The dog is tired.

Garnet: Please let Karl know your decision. I will be in touch with him. Thank you for coming.

Cant: Thank you for your courtesy and interest. Good day.

## 33 Adjusting to Temporal Love

"I will not go with you on another paper chase! I just won't. Not back east to some dreary humid southern red-neck backwater."

I realized I might have made a mistake, talking about going into another program in Georgia. I tried to hug her but she brushed my arms away. She did not react well, to say the least. I have been pleading my case like a lawyer without any evidence, rapidly and passionately, but without hope of forgiveness for the crime (speaking the truth? Or wanting to go?). Her retreat was immediate and uncompromising. I wonder if she had heard similar words before, perhaps with different meaning. I know I must prepare new supplications, but I am tired, "Gina, I love you. I hope you know that. I don't know how to be around you now—should I be always happy, to cheer you up? Or miserably depressed to let you know I share your state? Should I agree to stay? Or present the advantages of going together?"

"I have decided to go away, too. I applied for a scholarship in Art at Oregon. I asked for a two-year leave of absence from the library. I have to think of myself, now."

"What? Did you do that in secret? Why not tell—"

"You are pushing me out of your life like a raisin in a rising mass of dough. The swelling importance of everything else in your life reduces me to a wrinkled little fruit. Your mistake, if I am a fool and you are wise, except for this, was in emphasizing the singular importance of your program to the life of our relationship, as though nothing else could remedy our deteriorating alliance."

I was thinking that I could only write poetry sometimes, but she could speak it better than writing it. "But, together—"

"I want fame, success. I do not see how I could get either with you. You have no goals, no direction, just some strange kind of endurance."

"If you were famous, would you come back? If your name were on the lips of the rich and eminent, would it matter if it was on mine as well? Your name is on my lips, as if its incantation could produce you here, and you would listen and hear what you wanted and have it be enough to still your hunger."

"I don't know how I will remember you, perhaps I am too theatrical and amplify each hurt to outrageous proportions, but that is me, I don't know how to be different. How could I be so insecure, but then perhaps it isn't insecurity, but a furious and desperate wish to maintain the ethereal and spiritual as well as the practical elements in a love relationship. If love is entirely a secular and prosaic thing, then what of it, and I cannot lessen my own demands on discovering that the person in whom I love has ceased to love emotionally. When things become intellectual, then something else is dismissed. I have reached that stage, and I have to dismiss your love."

"If you want," I begged, "I won't ask you to be with me, until you indicate you want to be. I need you—not to live, or to be happy or pleasured—hey, clam shells can be separated and still live—but for emotional and spiritual fulfillment. I am a rare and precious cup, but useless without fluid or an observer—you are rare and precious liquid, but formless. Should the two not be combined to be actualized? That is what I really want."

"It is not enough! You have already left me. You are planning to be without me. You are frozen and glacial. You are a lord of ice. All your inflorescence is internal, as though in incubating an idea. You have a radical detachment to which all distractions are irritants that make you calm with boreal disdain, leaving a thicker shield of rime about yourself until you are wholly within your intellect, that mysterious machine-like capsule which could fling you far away at any time. Goodbye!"

"There's nothing I can say to impress you? Nothing I can say to soothe your pain? There's nothing I can say to inspire you to change? There's nothing I can say to make you believe that I accept you. There's nothing I can say to teach you serenity, there's nothing I can say to reach you, there's nothing I can say. Nothing."

"Nothing. It's over. My executive decision. I *have* to do this. You don't seem to know what you have to do!"

Nothing, I thought. I walked away, seeing everything bleed from me as I walked. So this is how intellectuals break up? I had expected more screaming, maybe welcomed it. She had screamed so many times about my decisions, about my detachment. Maybe she was right about both. After all, I am thinking this instead of screaming.

## 34 *Misfits in Armor: An Open Letter to the University Community*

19 June 1976

*Daily Simplotter Editor:*
As long as the university was rigid, careless, heartless and slow, it was possible to secure an education of sorts. If it turns out to be dishonest and incompetent as well, education may be very well impossible. Certainly fundamental questions are raised by my experience, which is not isolated by any means.

Most of the professors involved in my case are fairly well educated themselves, mostly competent and generally honest, with endearing personalities. Alas, they made a number of small mistakes or misjudgments. Rather than admit that or correct them, they and the administration have indulged in an obvious cover-up. In spite of my charges and offer to provide written evidence, no one has even examined it, much less made a judgment. The university's entire effort has gone into avoiding the issue.

Some of the faculty and administration are acting like medieval knights striving to prevail in a jousting match, padding themselves with heavier degrees and thicker publications, sharpening their tongues for clever combat. Nowhere is any wisdom exhibited. Education becomes a foolish struggle: students are taught ambition instead of contemplation and competition instead of cooperation.

At first, I was angry with you, because you smugly cemented your armor with insensitivity and ignorance to defend yourself from the truth, but now, having glimpsed, through a crack in the armor, naked, little worms, chained to each other's fear, I can only offer compassion. I know your insecurity, and I understand your fear. I cannot get anyone to read my thesis officially; and I cannot get a job for which I am qualified.

Perhaps you could have been forced to admit and correct the errors through some judicial process, but you probably would not have changed. Understanding cannot be forced. In that sense, I have wasted my own time attempting to force the university to follow its own code of ethics. The university must become self-examining and self-correcting on its own. Thus far it has failed sadly. I can no longer contend with the university over these matters. The university has senseless power, and has exercised it over people like myself, who have none, and can do nothing.

Others are afraid to become involved. Finn, Carson, and Kraft are afraid to admit their mistakes. Faculty hearing boards are afraid to find them mistaken. Strand and Garnet are afraid of backing the 'wrong' side, not knowing the truth themselves. If you will not admit it, then how can they? They are not brave enough to seek the truth.

## The Thesis

In spite of this struggle the university is dull—many of the students are, most of the faculty are, and all but two of the administrators are. I think it's dull because of the preoccupation with security and academic gamesmanship. I myself am fairly quiet and dull, but on this campus, I appear to be a raving radical. Simplotville is advertised as the "city with a smile," therefore Idaho Modern must be the "university with a smile." I pray it is the smile of Yeats' 'gay old chinaman' and not the vacuous reflex of idiocy by an inbred, brain-damaged ephemeromorph.

If my thesis diverges too much from the area of traditional philosophy, it is because it is, as Whitehead expected his philosophy to be, an adventure of ideas. If the metaphors stretch too far to hold, perhaps they are, as Wittgenstein wrote of his propositions, all nonsense, to be read and left behind.

You are afraid of being censured for your mistakes in my thesis. As Chuang Tsu said, "These who justify their faults to avoid punishment are many..." I am sorry that you count yourselves with the many. Chuang Tsu had sayings also that apply to us all: "Making accusations is not as good as laughing." And "laughter is not as good as letting things follow their natural course. Be content with what is happening." Perhaps I can be wise enough to be content. And to laugh about it. Can you?

Walter Cant

The local theater

## 35 Dream Future Hell

Gina is staying with a friend until I move out. This is unnecessary as I have the studio in the basement for $20 a month. I could sleep there at night. The first floor separates our rooms. After writing my letters, I just shoved over some clothes and lay on the bed to sleep.

The last dream: In Italy to visit Petko. In the dark industrial city everyone speaks English. Mitko and I visit his apartment. It is large but the floors are made of uneven dirt. There is a sink and stove in one corner, two cats. Old decayed laundry over chairs. In another corner a permanent wood fire. We talk; he lies down top of me in a strange hug.

Now in Russia, we decide to look for Ivan. We cannot find him. Go back to someone's apartment. He goes off; a friend of his comes. We go outside and look for things to sell. In a pile of clothes we find car keys and old written papers. We go back with the keys and wait in apartment.

Mitko sees Petko's father in the street and goes out. The streets are not level with waste and compacted trash. It is like entropy world, where everything is running downhill and cannot be cleaned or ordered. We cannot catch up with his father, who keeps disappearing around corners. Finally Mitko decides we would stop by his own apartment to ask where Petko is.

As we approach up a side street, we smell burning wood. The entrance has been covered by smoldering plywood, but we squeeze inside. The apartment has been turned into a rendering plant on a large scale. We wander around looking for the father. No one stops us, but continues working. There are piles of fish and small whales. Mitko picks out a sawn wolf skull and says vulk. I nod. There is one conveyor belt with an octopus and fish piled, moving towards a shredder. I turn around and see a squeezer, that is stripping and mashing a walrus into stringy blubber and flesh. I see a dead dolphin piled in the corner behind the machine. There seems only a slight odor and not a gagging smell.

We go to look at another machine. I sense a quiet presence behind us and see a quietly threatening man, who says nothing but raises his eyebrows, I say 'chaka malka' and tap Mitko on the shoulder. The guy leads us back to the entrance. The floors are uneven, the machines resting on centuries of waste. No one looks at us. They just seem to be moving around carrying body parts, maybe because I do not follow any one person to see where they go.

At the entrance, he goes down another hall, where a guard, unarmed is standing before another plywood door. They bend it back and motion for us to enter. Mitko does, but I see a few laborers and three or four army officers or policemen in light brown uniforms. I suddenly understand that these people are going to die soon and give up their flesh to the process. I refuse to go in. They both move towards me ordering me in. I turn and run, squeezing by the outer cardboard.

On the street the day to me to move in or they will kill me and leave me standing in the street. I start running downhill. The shorter more muscular guard starts after me. I can hear his breathing at my back. I briefly consider stopping to fight or tripping him. Then put everything into running. He drops back a little and starts threatening. We are running downhill in the dark, on crowded streets. People halt out of our way. I hit a pothole and my ankle starts to turn but I stretch my stride and run out of it. Now we are both running down the dark streets. I start to pull away—years of night running. People are throwing themselves to the ground as we run and we leap over them without breaking stride. He hits one of the prostrate people and stops to kill them. I hear the screams but do not look. I slow down and walk then throw myself to the ground when I hear him. He rushes past me. I get up and walk at an angle. He enters a square clean factory, must be energy generation. I can hear his voice as he makes an angry call.

I walk down another street, away from the building. I am totally lost, but I have been since I arrived. Nothing looks familiar. People are too busy and zombie-esque to talk to me. The city is strange. Apartments are tacked on too larger dirty brick buildings. Most have few windows and less glass. A woman shouts at me from one small broken window as if she knows me. I ignore her and walk away, ever downhill.

It is morning and I think to myself that I stayed the night with a woman, but have no memory or her, or where, or what happened. I am still walking downhill hoping desperately to get outside the city and rest on grass. The buildings have changed. They seem less dirty. There is more heat. No edge in site. I sit on a sloping sidewalk, more like another kind of track. I am watching a strange giant silver wormlike engine with a mandible crawling towards something warm. Heat is like I think. Are they alive? I see another. It is hotter. Nothing pays attention to me. I see another that has an articulate round body like a worm …

## 36  In the Forest

Saw 5 eagles just south of Salem, Oregon, driving to my summer job. Well, I made it after 15 hours of driving. I got lost about a mile from Hidden Valley forest (obviously a descriptive name). It started raining an hour before I got there. It was dark in the camping area and driving rain. I tried to set up the tent under a cedar, but a piece was missing and it collapsed. I just threw it over and slept in the back of the car, in a fetal position—now I can't stand straight. In the morning I was alone—no one else was here! So I walked to Edward's about a mile up a dirt road. He was eating breakfast, but immediately helped me fix a tent coupler out of an old conduit, so I went back and put up the tent for the next week.

The first week was like a vacation. We have been eating over a camp fire every night (sort of like camping, except for the work from 8 to 5). Sara, Heather and I built a table out of mill scraps (a portable mill was set up to cut on site) last week for food preparation. Terry and I set up a tent to keep food on. Keith and I went swimming every morning about 7, up the lake and back, past herons roosting on driftwood snags, with hawks circling, and fish nibbling our hairs sometimes (Bass?). The three girls came to swim also, but half an hour later, to maintain propriety (no one had a suit). I loved swimming there; I should go there every summer. The plums were ripe, and the orchard was by the lake, so for breakfast we had plums from the tree.

The second week, Peter came, and I showed everyone how to set up their chainsaws. Peter dropped a tree almost perfectly, but was irritated that the top was an inch off the target; I dropped one about 8 inches off, but I was very happy with that. Peter will help Edward finish this cut (one every 10 years) next month. Fred and Shirley bought and fixed a salmon dinner last night, especially good compared to peanut butter and lettuce.

In the forest, I dug a ditch to see who was living underground. Brought my magnifying glass. Ditch looked like a grave—sudden daymare that I was going to be arrested as a serial killer preparing his next site. Went back to looking at fungus, so light, so intricate. Perhaps this is Being as being that the philosophers droned about. My vocabulary is eroding and being replaced. Yikes.

Good walk in the forest.  Life at the bottom of the atmosphere, through distortions of light, which is what colors were.  What was sunlight without colored wings? What was the wind without an occasional song to carry?  What was silence without a chattering of life to surround it, for on the solar scale, it was silence that surrounds life.

Lying on the moss, after another hour of crawling, I thought that maybe my life with Gina was like the phosphorus cycle between the atmosphere, earth's crust, and oceans. Only information from her eroded into my interior oceans, where much of it lay inert; some moved back to land where it supported plants, decomposers and animals—the problem was that I could not know all the information at once—just wait for its release.

As I was laying here thinking, I heard "gack gack gack" from the forest, getting closer. Then a large pileated woodpecker buzzed me twice before settling on the elderberry bush, hanging upside down, eating alcoholic berries, gacking at me sometimes to let me know he was very alert; I knew he was a helpless drunk, so I just laughed and watched. And he gacked and watched back out of one eye. Work slowed down and I lay in the grass.

I finally solved the old philosophical riddle: If a tree falls in the forest and nobody is around to hear it, does it make a sound? Duh, yes. It makes waves, and virtually everyone in the forest, from trees to beetles and owls, can hear it. No humans required, just living beings. Philosophy makes up ridiculous questions and still gets the debated answers wrong.

After a few weeks of being cradled by cedar roots, I rehabilitated a cabin that had been abandoned since 1970, when the commune broke up. I slept almost well, almost 8 hours a night. It was comfortable (I found a drier bed and threw out the old one here). I was staying at in a cabin in the woods (Hidden Valley was 420 acres and was a certified demonstration ecoforest that they had been planning for over 3 years now and operating for over 1); the cabin was almost identical to Gina's father's old studio. It had 8 white wooden double-hung windows. Inside the walls were all knotty pine, with a 10-foot plaster ceiling. It was all one room with a fireplace and kitchen at one and bed and armoire at the other. In the middle I had desk, computer, bookcases, and dining table with the old Sanyo stereo and French table cloth on it. I bought a wool carpet for the floor. The kitchen had a tiny refrigerator and a propane stove, but nice carpentered cabinets. The sink had running water that came from a garden hose in the stream above the cabin. There was an outhouse in back and solar shower down the trail (actually cleaner than the one in Paris in *The Razor's Edge*). It was extraordinarily quiet.

So quiet that I could not bring myself to play the stereo the first 2 nights. One night, however, I put on Tchaikovsky's 5th, which I found was worn out. Just as well, I didn't have enough fluids left to cry for a whole symphony—of course I thought of you and that long moment when—Surely if I had a heart left, it would have broken at the second movement. So, I worked at the computer for a while. As I was working a large curious lizard came out from under the stove. As I reached to pick him (her?) up, he scuttled back under—this happened 2 more times. After I went to sleep, he probably had the run of the room. The cabin is surrounded by trees, mostly Ponderosa pine and pencil cedar (so called because used in No.2 pencils), with a few white fir and arbutus, a deciduous oak-like tree we didn't have in Idaho; there are many shrubs, mostly willow and alder, and many flowers and herbs, including daisy, Oregon grape, and poison oak.

I saw an eagle today, a few crows and owls yesterday. Two big alligator lizards outside the cabin. Heard a coyote, but haven't seen one; their song is different in Oregon than Idaho, but probably not as different as from the clans in Illinois or Georgia.

Another hard day began at 6 a.m. Marty, our resident expert, started the plant survey early. This survey was to flag the native grasses for the oak-pine savanna restoration project; many were the same as in the Palouse, mostly fescues like Idaho or red fescue. So we flagged for 3-4 hours. The ceanothus was blooming its rich blue sprays. Ox-eye daisies were everywhere. Even cat's ears were everywhere there.

I became a pack animal. For instance, in the vest that Gina bought for me as a going away present, I kept, in the front pockets: an altimeter, compass, map wheel, clinometer (for measuring slopes and tree heights), pocket knife, watch, ruler (for tree core measure), thermometer (for water temp.), prism (for counting trees in a 10th-acre), and lunch (2 breakfast bars). On the inside I carried a Tatum aid (plastic riparian codes), maps, plant id book, and toilet paper. In the back pocket, I carried an increment borer and an aluminum notebook with waterproof survey forms—I thought that was funny at first, but Friday through Tuesday, it rained and I had to fill out forms in the rain, so I was happy it was waterproof. On my belt I carried a two-chain tape measure (66 feet per chain, to measure each reach of a stream). I carried a biltmore stick and hipsometer. I had to wear my hard hat (legal requirement); I wore boots and 5 layers of clothing, from undershirt, shirt, sweatshirt, vest to raincoat (short yellow forester's). This stuff was heavy!

We were looking over the 40-acre valley at the center of the property. Marty was expounding on a burning plan, "My people have burned these valleys for ten thousand years, to drive animals and to select good species to eat. These ecosystems have become man-made, and unique species have developed. Men would set fires at the bottom of the slopes and let them burn to the tops, where they burned out."

We asked a few questions about plants and Snake listed a few, "Morrell mushrooms. They grow in places from here to Seattle and west. Native peoples burned all those grasslands, we created all those by burning."

"Not all," I said automatically.

"All!" He emphasized, maybe not used to being contradicted, "Name one that wasn't."

"Uhmmm, the Palouse grassland is a mature grassland not maintained by fire."

"Yes, it was," he said without pause, "my Nez Perce brothers burned it annually."

"No, they didn't. If they had, it would have killed the native species."

"Lentils and wheat are not native."

"I was referring to Idaho fescue and bearberry, which are native. Even the Artemisia species cannot be burned."

"Have you ever lived there?"

"Yes, have you?"

"No, but I know the land. My people have been living for thousands—"

"You're people were fighting the Norwegians for—"

"No, I am Native, my father—"

"Your mother was Swedish, your father was Mexican, your grandmother—"

"Who told you that? My grandmother was Chumash."

"And, you were born in Santa Barbara. I was born in Portland and I'm as native as you. It's just that my parents adopted new ways and left the old behind."

"They were fools, like you," Snake stalked off and walked up into the woods.

Jack pushed my shoulder, "Don't set him off. We need his help. Perhaps you could be more humble. And, don't tell me I told you his ancestry. Or I'll be upset."

"We can finish the walk and figure some of it out," I offered.

The next day, as I started driving into town for some bread and peanut butter, Snake stopped me. I rolled down the window.

"Get out," he said, "we need to talk."

I said, "I'm comfortable sitting. What shall we talk about?"

"Fahhh," he said and walked off.

At the Sunday common meal, I asked Snake to help me with the plant survey near the old growth area 3. He agreed, so we started just after light, about 6 a.m. the next day. We only spoke plant names and wrote notes for the first half an hour. Finally, I offered, "I apologize for suggesting that you were mostly Swedish. I understand that when you have parents and relatives of different cultures, you should be free to choose which will be your identity."

He nodded but did not reply. I continued, "I have known some very white people who chose to be native, or black, or oriental—it did not seem to fit."

He nodded again and after a while said, "You cannot choose your parents, but you can choose, a wise person, can choose a good culture. Why didn't you?"

"I chose a culture of ideas. It was never important to me whether my parents or theirs were thieves or nobility."

"Which were they?"

"Thieves, I think, at first, then railroad men and wives. My father was an engineer."

Marty smiled for the first time in days, "You're wrong about burning in the Palouse, also."

"No, I can prove that, if you are open to reality. But, you are right about the Umpqua people burning these hills. I can see the differences in composition."

"We can agree to disagree perhaps."

"Nonsense, you are a scientist. One of us is more correct in some things then the other."

"Perhaps we can finish this survey and have beans tonight. My woman started a new pot this morning. Then we can discuss this in comfort."

"Thank you, I'd like that. My grandfather married a Chinook woman."

He looked at me and said, "I can see that."

"No you can't," I said. "I look like a German with Greek and French blood. And, your blond hair is not characteristic of a Chumash."

"It will be greyer soon. Don't step on the Oregon grape there."

I wrote down the grape, then he pointed out a bird's nest. We walked up the slope towards the top of the hill.

"The Nez Perce did burn," he stated.

"I am aware they burned fires for cooking, but their fires did not shape the grassland. Neither did grazing bison, who had moved east of the Rockies. That grassland was shaped by climate."

"I see you persist in your errors."

"Error is always possible, but the best science shows climate and geology are, or were, the controlling factors."

"Perhaps when you have a better feel of—"

And so our discussion continued through the survey and through dinner, until his wife and son asked us to go outside so they could see the movie.

I was beginning to wonder if I was the last rational person in this state also, the only one not warped by pride or not too defensive and too insecure to be wrong or to learn. I was thinking that he was proud of his heritage and proud of his knowledge, but seemed to resist knowledge that contradicted what he wanted to be true. I on the other hand I thought was open to learning new things, which is why I wanted his help in this forest that I did not know.

The camping aspects, which were mildly fascinating the first month, now were just habits; solar showers, outhouses, cooking over an open fire (veggie dogs and crackers, or peanut butter cold). Still, in the outhouse I had been letting the spiders come back; one spun her web right over the ash bucket, so I made a small hole in the south side of the web so I could scoop the ashes every other day (to cover the fallen excrement); another spun hers between the hole and the pit, a very large web cunningly engineered to catch flies who try to get down—unfortunately, every falling turd broke the center, so she had rewoven it on 3 sides; finally, spiders had woven webs in every corner. There was enough room for all of us, though.

Marty and I had some good conversations, mostly about preservation, native practices and native plants. Jack, Anne and I had good conversations about philosophy and building techniques—they may help me put a porch on the cabin next month, then insulate the north wall with hay bales. It seemed like a lot of work for two months stay.

Jack decided that I might be better suited to interface with the Hispanic crew, rather than rile up Marty. The crew was mostly unemployed loggers or dropouts needing conservation training. They were mostly young but very serious. They asked a lot of questions about the forest. The training was only two days before we were assigned.

Then we met with the BLM crew to finish conducting the stream surveys on BLM land in the Sears Creek watershed. My group got satellite maps and had to "truth" the streams on the ground; a computer used elevation algorithms to plot where streams ought to be, but often it showed old logging roads and missed new streams or those under heavy vegetative cover. I am the only one over 30—maybe that was why I was the leader. We tracked through heavy brush the day taking readings and measurements; my job is to identify riparian plant associations.

The second day was worse because it was raining all day. I was soaked before 8 a.m. Some other BLM crew came by later, but did not get out of their new government trucks. We had lunch about 1 p.m.—I had a banana and 2 crackers. There are still some Oregon plants I could not identify, even knowing the associational plants. There were many beautiful pencil cedar and Douglas-fir trees, large, but not as large as some of the trees that had fallen (5-feet across); there was salal, Oregon grape, trailing blackberry, beargrass, sword ferns, old man's beard, sedges, fescues, mosses, and Columbia brome, twinflower, and many more. There was some true old-growth structure, which made it hard to walk. We also saw a few fingerlings (cutthroat trout), salamanders, centipedes, a rabbit, and a large pile of mountain lion dung.

I noticed, as we went out in the forest, the animals and birds sort of receded away from us in a wave, only the turkey vultures seemed to ignore us, or rather watch for our demise. Deer trails abounded; coyotes yapped in the evening. Sometimes, I caught sight of a dusky-footed wood rat or a junco sneaking out of a nest—but, had not seen a bear or mountain lion yet.

The third day we got into the old-growth. It was so beautiful, I called a break every hour for 15-20 minutes. To get there, though, we had to hike down a 65% steep hill of clearcut—nothing left but a few hardwoods and many tall thorny shrubs and 6-foot high sword ferns (the BLM had it clearcut about 12 years ago). We were soaking wet before 7:30 a.m.—except Erardo, who wore rubber boots and rain clothes (logger gear is expensive but popular here). The streams in the cut areas were overgrown with ferns, but had no shade trees; there was a lot of erosion uphill.

In the old growth there was hardly any understory; the large trees (called legacy or grandparent trees, depending on who you talked to) were spaced quite far apart and were quite huge—larger than anything we have, and taller. When Erardo asked what class of tree it was, I answered, "TFH, I believe."

He nodded and wrote it down.

I said, "Yup, Totally Fucking Huge is a real class."

Two of the guys with better English laughed, but when I tried to repeat it in Spanish, they all laughed. I thought my Spanish was actually decent.

This streams had salamanders and fish (possibly trout but very small and very fast); there were snakes, deer, bear, centipedes in evidence. The kinnikinnik and salal were in bloom; both had small globe-shaped white flowers. I heard a few Steller's jays.

Then, as we walked to the 4th stream, we heard two owls. Victor asked what they were and I said horned owls. As I lay down on the moss for lunch, a large shape glided up and landed in a tanoak—no sound, just movement. It watched us. Rene asked if it was a horned owl—I said no, too small, no horns. It was spotted with black eye markings; the book said a spotted owl—none of us had ever seen one before. Not having a mouse or squirrel, I held up a piece of English muffin, and motioned for Erardo to take a picture (with the BLM stream camera). He got within 10 feet and took a few pictures. Then Rene and I went over. We talked to him (or her); tried to offer food. I held up a branch for him to perch on. After 30 minutes, we had to continue working, but he followed us, once landing within 5 feet (for a few more pictures, no doubt). A small owl spotted all over, with beautiful wings and eyes, tiny beak and huge claws. Rene asked if that meant that the land would be taken off any possible sale—I said yes, and laughed, adding so might some private lands bordering it. Naturally I wrote it up immediately, suggesting that there might be 2-3 nesting couples in the area.

The stream itself was quite different from the outer ones. It was almost all cobble, with little gravel, sand or clay. It was layered for thousands of feet like an exquisite Japanese garden. Pieces of wood, from dead snags, made little dams and pools; water meandered over rock and wood, around rock and mossy banks. Huge trees towered up through the canopy and subcanopy, through delicate vine maples, past occasional clumps of grass, and flowering salal. Except for the fact I was tired, wet, and scratched to shreds, I was very happy there.

## The Thesis

When I got back to the cabin I fell asleep without eating. I was awakened by a low whooshing noise. The I saw the shape of a bat. I jumped up and opened the front door, but she was enjoying going back and forth from end to end and didn't leave. Many moths and a spider did come in, however, so I closed the door again. Finally the bat settled down by the bicycle helmet and I was able to go back asleep. When I woke up, she had gone out the way she had come in. The blue jays had built a nest outside in the eastern eave—it was rare for them to put a nest in a building, although it was only 20 yards from an older abandoned nest; maybe it was the young jay's first nest. Now, I could watch them fly by the window all day.

The fourth day was similar, except that there was no spotted owl. In the later afternoon, however, we stumbled across many potted marijuana plants, so I ended the day early and we backed out quickly, just in case it was actively protected. As I was walking back to the cabin in the dark, the moon was full and incredibly bright—more incredibly because it was just reflected light. Bars of light divided the trail, which was overgrown with tall trees (Douglas-fir mostly) and very dark. I was parallel to a long field that ran down the valley that was completely lit; the grasses seemed to glow. The coyotes were howling—I figured they just liked to play in moonlight, not really howl at the moon. I saw a small bat flitter beneath the trees. I was completely lost for a while. Was it the same planet? Everything looked and felt different. Watching. Living. Breathing. Reflecting. I stood in the yard by the cabin finally and looked at the pock-marked moon.

Cant in the Hidden Valley Forest

To think, I was almost one of the dry-balls of academe. Maybe Ellsin said that, I cannot remember. The summer, which had stretched so long ahead of me, was now almost all behind me. I had arranged for my last paycheck to be sent to the department in Georgia. In truth, I did not want to leave. Maybe I would screw up my next academic exercise, and I could come back and just do this for the rest of my life.

## 37 Down to Georgia

The 'Deathmobile' scared off many drivers, so I often had the back roads to myself. It wasn't that bad actually. It was a 1964 Mercury Comet. Both bumpers had been bumped savagely, but still protected the metal. The hood and trunk lid had rusted badly. Whenever I checked the oil and dropped the hood, there was a shower of red particles. If I put small items in the side of the trunk, they would fall out over the highway, so everything had to be wrapped in sheets to keep it inside. The front windshield leaked when it rained. The seats were wrecked. But the engine and transmission seemed to be immortal. Best $200 I ever spent.

I spent the entire trip rehearsing what I had done wrong in Idaho and everything I could do right in Georgia. I rattled through Atlanta and then on to Athens. I wonder how much the name of the city had to do with my decision. No, I wanted to study ecosystem ecology and this was the center of thought in that area. Eugene Odum had just written an article linking optimum populations to the size and productivity of ecosystems.

When I got on campus and found the building, I parked in a Visitors space and went inside. As I was approaching the office, a young lady, obviously an undergraduate student, asked if I was Mr. Cant. I said yes, in fact, I was.

She introduced herself, "My name is Mandy. The department has asked me to show you around, where you will be staying, where the classrooms and the labs are, and afterwards to drive you out to the research forest."

"Well, thank you, I am flattered and grateful," and gave a slight bow. Where had that came from—oh, must be the Germanic heritage.

We took the Deathmobile. I was sure she was impressed with its ability to move quietly. The rooms were quads, four rooms sharing a common living room and kitchen. It only took us two trips to move in everything I owned, or was owned by. We left my car, at her request, and walked around the campus. My immediate advisor would be Dean Carabissian, but he was not in his office just then, so we left a message. Mandy said that because of my Spanish and supervisory skills, I would be working with a Hispanic cooperative on a thinning project. I knew then that Georgia people had been in close contact with the Oregon people. I wondered what they thought about the Idahohummer people. Then she drove me out to the forest, with my sleeping bag, vest and notebook. I would be working on thinning on weekends. Then, during the week, I would taking the classes I needed to fatten up deficiencies. Alas, I was always deficient in some area.

## 38 In the Pines

The Hispanic Cooperative workers came today to work on slash removal and ladder fuel removal. I was wondering if that was why the trees were called slash pines. The work was fast and easy; these guys were professional. After a whirlwind of cutting, we set up lunch—two giant pots of beans. My culinary contribution was a loaf of "dry white toast," which everyone but me and Julio ignored. I barely remembered anyone's name. In the afternoon the whirlwind continued. I got very tired of working fast. The pace of life seemed faster in the East, regardless of culture.

Monday and Tuesday, there were no classes, so I went for walks in the research forest. The first animal I came across was a garter snake with its twin racing stripes. I tried to pick her up, but she led me into various thickets so I just watched. This is the third kind of snake I saw in an hour. Earlier, I tracked a bull snake through the grass, also called gopher snake because he eats gophers (as well as birds and chipmunks). He vibrated kind of like a rattlesnake, but was eager to get away (and I was relieved not to get bitten). In fact the only snake not eager to get away from me was the first, a rubber boa today, who wrapped around my wrist when I picked her up sunning herself on the road—rubber boas are easy to tell sex; the female lacks small claw-like grips (left-over leg relicts) near the anus. She felt like rubber. She was olive brown and drab, like the male, with a thick tail. By the way they really do kill mice by constriction, just like their big relatives, boa constrictors. Anyway, I put her on a rock away from the road, with a stern lecture. I hope to find a kingsnake here someday; they look like coral snakes but have black stripes, as well as red and white, and they are not poisonous.

Tuesday, I came across a painted turtle, basking on a trail. She was pretty far from the stream. I played with her a while, just looking mostly; she had red net-like lines on her carapace, and red and yellow stripes on her legs and neck. When she got too unhappy I put her back next to the trail where she could hide under leaves. I have never seen a turtle here before. I was worried that they had disappeared (they are just to interesting to not play with).
    Maybe she was after fresh leaves or fungus (it had just rained the day before). Unlike humans and some mammals, female box turtles (painteds are in the box turtle family) take much longer to mature than males. Their courtship is quite elaborate, although I've only read about it; they face each other and the male strokes her head and neck with a foreclaw.
    I saw a coyote on the trail, later. We played hide and seek for a while (that is

I played—he moved away warily but was curious). A beautiful brown and very graceful. The birds were active, but no snakes that day.

Back at the dorm, I started another article on spirituality and sacred forests—the Latin word *templum*, from which we get temple, used to mean a forested area that had been separated off to be kept sacred; temples were just closed-in forests, with pillars, which themselves used to represent wisdom in the form of sacred trees, such as oak and laurel. For the Greeks, each God was associated with a particular tree, e.g. Apollo with Laurel or Pan with pines. Well, and so on, blah, blah blah. I have to prepare a talk for later, so this was practice.

The next weekend, ah, just another day of work—a few more cuts and scratches—two on my face from branches. I met with Morten from the Three Pines Institute; we were to set up a demonstration next month. Xavier and the Hispanic crew were working at the same time Morten and I were, so we took a break together. In a funny scene reminiscent of *Mountains of the Moon*, we all compared scars. I had a dramatic long cut on my left shin, still scabbing, but it was superficial and everyone booed when I showed it. Julio had a real great scar on his shoulder from a large falling branch. Alain had a scar across his forehead from a truck crash. Emilio easily won the 'contest' with missing fingers, and chainsaw scars on his shoulder, face, and leg—he is either the sloppiest forest worker I've known or the luckiest. They invited us to lunch on burritos, so we talked about trucks and saws.

Sunday was a quiet day working in the forest. One of my small pet projects was to restore old growth structure to an even-aged forest. So, I spent time looking over the pattern of trees. I cut down a medium sized tree so that it fell sideways across the slope of the hill—that tree would be allowed to rot in place; it could hold up to five times as much water as a standing tree; fungi, plants and insects would use it; it would block water flowing down the slope, changing the hydrological regime and soil topography. I also pushed a stump over, so it would create a pit and mound topography. It would not be the same as natural development, but it might protect the soil better.

Monday, I had to refocus quickly on the demo project. So, I spent more time hauling poles to the demo site. In the rain. As I was dragging one pole (they weigh 60-90 kilograms), I looked down and saw a huge bear print. I kept looking over my shoulder all afternoon. Then after I quit, I was walking by a fruit tree, when I saw a bear cub in an apple tree; the mother was standing just under the tree; the cub looked at me, I looked at the mother, the mother looked at the cub. I kept walking, praising their choice of apples. This bear was only a 45-gallon size. Funny that none of the local dogs was barking. I was too tired to have run, or barked, anyway.

## The Thesis

Tuesday, we set up the portable test mill and ran a hundred poles through it. I think my arms were coming out of their sockets from lifting logs. The television station was there and I was running poles through while he was filming, so I was probably be on television. Someone else had a video camera and was taking film. Great, I was dressed to the neck in three layers of wool, sweating, wearing a hard-hat with face mask and ear protectors, and then I got coverage!

The mill was a giant orange breadbox on wheels. It was made in Canada. The poles went in one side and lumber came out the other. Inside were four chipper heads and 3 head saws. It cost $140,000, but we were probably not going to buy it. This test used all the poles that we cut anyway. Xavier was here, and many other people from the Three Pines Institute. Afterwards, we went out for a Mexican lunch.

Classes were more relaxed than I thought. It was almost as though everyone thought I knew what I was doing. I was looking here for someone to help me improve my Spanish, or as Dean said, my Mexican. Dean pointed out that he had learned Spanish in Spain, and it was very different from what the Hispanic crew spoke. I could sympathize with a fellow elitist, but I needed to communicate more than be proper. I thought I might take piano lessons again one evening a week.

Friday night, I walked up the hill in the forest with my sleeping bag and matches. Found a really soft patch of moss, lit a small fire, and camped out. During the night I heard a rustling, then a shuffling, so I started singing praises to the local bear. As soon as I spoke, a brown beast came running up to the sleeping bag and jumped! It was Emilio's dog, who had followed my scent. I finally got her to lie down and be quiet—she only barked twice. It was very quiet, not even an owl. When I woke up, I was cool, so I walked downhill, with the remarkably quiet dog, and sat at an old picnic table waiting for the crew. Emilio should be happy to see his dog.

I thought that I did not know what I desired, success or quiet. Money or time in the woods. The word desire meant that the object was out of reach. Only luck and hope could help with desire, not will or money. Furthermore, effort was required. (Desire was from the root word 'sueid,' meaning to shine or glow; it had the same root as star, 'sidus'). Desideratum was the object, of course, sometimes showing in dreams. The original Germanic word for dream, 'dhreugh,' described music and joy and wondrous visions. But, it was derived from the Sanskrit, 'druhyati,' meaning hurts or deceives. Oh, no, the academic virus was nascent again.

## 39 All Sweetness and Light

I decided to write a letter to Gina, knowing that it might be refused, rejected or ignored. So, I wrote:

Sweetness and Light:

Honey bees are "all sweetness and light," Horace said. Remember, that is why I called you that instead of the meaningless 'honey' or 'dear.'

I was thinking about the aesthetics of forests; must be leftover philosophy dregs. Did you know that most trees twist one way or another; redwoods twist the same direction as their parent trees. Scots pine twists depending on the rockiness of the soil. Jeffrey pine twists with prevailing winds. Heat stress causes right hand spirals in Slash pine here in Georgia. Old folk knowledge says that right-handed spirals in Douglas-fir are caused by right-winged owls sitting in the trees watching the moon travel east.

When I fall to the ground I always turn left and land on my right-hand shoulder—but what if I had an owl on that shoulder or if the moon wasn't up, like it is now. I know that you twist to the right in your sleep. Did you know that? I have two cats, now. They compete with mice for food; they don't hurt the mice directly. I have been noticing that they turn counterclockwise to lie down. Here is a picture of Aldous Huxley II and Maurice Merleau-Ponty II.

In my dream last night, our 5-year-old son (sorry, it's a dream, not reality) is taking his first airplane trip with me; he is sitting on my lap (blonde, blue-eyes). He is also drooling (think he has a cold) while he asks questions. Cute and intelligent. I can't remember where we were going or why we were on a plane. The dream ended when the refrigerator started breaking down. Hey, it was a dream. Must be the deepest levels of my body thinking of reproducing the patterns that are we.

Last night, I got tired of studying. It was too warm and I was sweating over the keyboard. So, I opened the door, sat on the top step and had a

## The Thesis

cigarette (yes, I also drink and cuss now—it all helps, damn it).

The rain was very gentle, but regular. The smoke curled up under the eave and mixed with the fog. Couldn't blow a good smoke ring at all. I dreamed last night that we went for a walk. That you came with me to a class somewhere (Idaho?). That you fell asleep during class—just like graduate school, huh? I sorted a few pictures before bed, then read part of a sci fi novel. Yawn.

I wonder if you wake at the same time?

Love

W

It took me two days to get it to a mailbox. I was going mad from living in the quads dorm, the constant noise and talking, all with no rhythm. I decided to look for a small studio further from the university, maybe in the town.

Two days of work in the forest. Dean and I worked (in the rain again). I took the digital camera again. We measured a lot of trees in ecozones 7 and 8. We cut down three trees to measure the crown, needles, and check for disease—funny that every science has to kill whatever it studies, like a mechanical Basilisk.

I saw another coyote on the second day. I wondered if it was not a gray fox, because it was smaller and did not seem to have a black-tipped tail (although foxes usually did).

It stopped raining. The moon was out and shined from behind the clouds, so that it was bright enough to see the trees and mountains. It was a very interesting quality of light, and it seemed that everything was very clear to me, and that I was so transparent that anyone could see the mountains through me.

## 40 Eclipse of the Earth by the Moon

September 5, 1984

It's over. Finally. The President of Idaho Modern University forcefully suggested that the Dean of the Graduate School had to send the thesis to external reviewers chosen by the Master's committee—actually they all were chosen by Professor Finn. Naturally he chose the most prestigious schools possible, Harvard, Chicago, and California, hoping no doubt ... ah, well. The thesis was approved at all three. The Harvard reviewer noted that it would have been awarded a Ph.D. at Harvard. The Chicago reviewer was a former President of the American Philosophical Society and the Department head. Ironically, the California reviewer was one that Walter had sent his thesis to as a book manuscript; despite suspicions of being tricked, and misgivings about the style, this reviewer reluctantly and eventually reaffirmed his previous recommendation.

The school however, at the demand of the Dean, withheld the diploma until Walter could take his orals. Walter asked who, if anyone, at the school is qualified to administer those orals. Poor Walter. Wittgenstein might have recognized that he was a genius, since he said "Genius is talent exercised with courage." Walter had both and a unique chance to exercise both. The President finally recognized that in 1979 and waived the orals, but there were hold-ups due to registration and library fines, which were not resolved for a while.

The biology department belatedly and formally refused to readmit Walter as a degree candidate, saying only that they had no one on the faculty who was expert enough in Walter's declared field: ecosystem productivity. By then, I doubt if Walter cared.

After a sparkling summer at Georgia, he got a graduate teaching fellowship there (although UG refused to recognize the unfinished Idaho degree), where he studied with his idol, Eugene Odum, apparently without discord to speak of. His Ph.D. was approved and granted in 1980. Idaho Modern mailed his M.A. diploma in 1981 (he sent me a copy of it, but it looked like it had dark smears on it, perhaps chocolate, perhaps not). He went to study wolves and Inupiat in Alaska for several years, but he was laid off, along with many others, when the budgets were cut in the mid-1980s. I heard that he was working on a tree farm in Montana and cutting firewood for a living.

The young Alcibiades had become a hard-drinking Socrates, pissing off people with questions about their values and styles of living, an honest, curious wanderer approaching the hemlock like a robin flying to a fermenting elderberry.

Caesar Finn, of course, retired with great honors, Leigh Carson published a book on Wittgenstein and Merleau-Ponty—two authors she had considerable difficulty with for a time—and was awarded a sabbatical to study Danish philosophers, and K. Ronn Kraft was made head of his department. The various members of the committees bored back into the university woodwork. President Garnet and Dean Strand retired happily to country homes.

Surprisingly, Walter and Dean Strand actually worked together by mail on a bibliography of forest insect pests until it was published five years later. As Wittgenstein said, "In philosophy the winner of the race is the one who can run most slowly. Or: the one who gets there last." Or perhaps just the one who outlasts the competition.

Even more surprisingly, Gina and Walter maintained a long distance relationship, writing and calling, then visiting each other every month or two. I think they still wrote or painted together. They seemed to really respect and treasure each other—but I confess I was a little jealous.

As for me, I found a great job in New York City, where I do little more than read and write. I visited Walter once in Montana, on the way to a conference back in Idaho. He treated me to a day of roughing it, slogging through snow, eating out of a frying pan over burning pinecones. I got a tour of the forest and took some great photos. He seemed at peace. My Thor is happy and at peace, too. Oh, and I still play with words, me, Ms. 'neon o mills,' breath strong with 'onion smell,' who works her own 'linen looms' at the 'solo elm inn,' not like an 'ill omen son,' but more like a 'solemn lion.'

The moral of Walter's story:

Being joyful is more important than being right.

Walter thinking

### *Colophon*

Text font: Adobe Garamond Pro
Display font: Gill Sans
Machinery: Mac G5 & HP Photosmart
Codes: Indesign, Acrobat & Photoshop
Photographs & Graphics: M. A. de Passe
Design:  A. M. Caratheodory

www.ingramcontent.com/pod-product-compliance
Lightning Source LLC
Chambersburg PA
CBHW031357040426
42444CB00005B/330